Baedeker's
BARCELONA

Imprint

96 colour photographs, 14 drawings, 15 plans, 1 general plan, 1 special plan, 1 transport plan, 1 large city map

Original German text: Peter M. Nahm, Ostfildern-Kemnat

General direction: Dr Peter Baumgarten, Baedeker, Stuttgart

English language edition: Alec Court

Cartography: Harms, Ingenieurbüro für Kartographie, Erlenbach; Falk Verlag, Hamburg (large city map)

Source of illustrations: Baedeker archive (4); Historia-Photo 1; Museu d'Història de la Ciutat (1); Nahm (77); Skupy (9); Ullstein (2)

English translation: David Cocking, Crispin Warren, Julie Waller

Following the tradition established by Karl Baedeker in 1844, sights of particular interest and hotels and restaurants of particular quality are distinguished by either one or two asterisks.

To make it easier to locate the various places listed in the "A to Z" section of the Guide, their co-ordinates on the large city map are shown at the head of each entry.

Only a selection of hotels, restaurants and shops can be given: no reflection is implied, therefore, on establishments not included.

In a time of rapid change it is difficult to ensure that all the information given is entirely accurate and up to date, and the possibility of error can never be entirely eliminated. Although the publishers can accept no responsibility for inaccuracies and omissions, they are always grateful for corrections and suggestions for improvement.

1st edition 1992

© Baedeker Stuttgart
Original German edition

© 1992 Jarrold and Sons Ltd
English language edition worldwide

© 1992 The Automobile Association
United Kingdom and Ireland

US and Canadian Edition Prentice Hall Press

Distributed in the United Kingdom by the Publishing Division of The Automobile Association, Fanum House, Basingstoke, Hampshire, RG21 2EA.

Licensed user:
Mairs Geographischer Verlag GmbH & Co., Ostfildern-Kemnat bei Stuttgart

Reproductions:
Gölz Repro-Service GmbH, Ludwigsburg

The name *Baedeker* is a registered trademark

Printed in Italy by G. Canale & C. S.p.A. – Borgaro T.se – Turin

ISBN 0–13–063561–8 US and Canada
      0 7495 0410 2 UK

Contents Page

The Principal Sights at a Glance

Preface

This pocket guide to Barcelona is one of the new generation of Baedeker guides.

These guides, in a convenient format, are illustrated throughout in colour, and are designed to meet the needs of the modern traveller. They are quick and easy to consult, with the principal places of interest described in alphabetical order. Practical details about hours of opening, how to get there, etc., are shown in the margin.

Barcelona, the capital of Catalonia, rivals Madrid not only on cultural and economic grounds, but also because of the extensive building and infrastructural preparations it is making for the Olympic Games in 1992.

The present guide is divided into three parts. The first part gives a general account of the city – including population, government, language, economy, transport and culture. This is followed by an account of some famous people who were natives of Barcelona or who have been associated with the city, and a survey of its history.
A selection of quotations and a brief account of Modernisme leads into the second part of the guide, in which the principal places of interest in Barcelona and its surroundings are described in alphabetical order. The third part, also arranged alphabetically, contains a variety of practical information, designed to help visitors to find their way about and make the most of their stay.

Baedeker guides concentrate on essential information and are user-friendly. This new guide is abundantly illustrated and contains a number of carefully revised plans and numerous colour photographs. At the back of the book is a comprehensive map and against each entry in the A to Z section are given the co-ordinates of the square of the map in which the particular feature can be located.

Facts and Figures

Arms of
Barcelona

General

Barcelona, the capital of the autonomous region of Catalonia (Catalunya), lies 2° 10' east (on the same meridian as Paris) and 41° 23' north, in the extreme north-east of the Iberian Peninsula.

Location

Favourably situated on a broad coastal plain rising gently from the sea up to Tibidabo, which is 532m/1746ft high, the city is bordered on the northeast by Muntanya Pelada and on the south-west by Montjuïc. On the far side of Muntanya Pelada lies the gorge of the Riu Besos, while south of Montjuïc the Riu Llobregat flows into a wide and fertile plain, the fruit and vegetable garden of Barcelona.

Not only is Barcelona the most important economic, communications, educational and cultural centre in Catalonia, it is also now competing successfully with Spain's capital city of Madrid in those fields. It boasts some distinguished colleges and other educational establishments, an archbishop, a large number of museums, some of international standing, important publishing-houses and is a stronghold of musical and theatrical life. Recently, too, it has become a centre of industrial design.

Importance

◀ Columbus Column at the Harbour

Features of the city

The face of the city has been moulded by three main phases in its history: the Roman period, extensive remains of which have been discovered beneath the medieval town centre; the mainly Gothic core of the city; and finally the large scale development undertaken in the 19th c. As Spain remained neutral in both World Wars and the Spanish Civil War (1936–39), violent though it was, did not result in large areas of destruction, Barcelona has survived well architecturally.

Old Town

The Old Town is bounded by the harbour and by wide inner ring-roads ("rondas") which have replaced the old walls. On the highest point in the city centre, Mont Tabor (12m/40ft high), stands the Cathedral, surrounded by narrow medieval alleyways. The main streets are the Ramblas, wide tree-lined promenades which divide the Old Town into two parts, Barri Gòtic and Barri Xino.

Eixample

The newer districts, the Eixample, with their boulevards lined with plane trees and their stately houses, have been built largely in accordance with plans drawn up around 1860, with the roads laid out to a formal grid pattern. At that time, too, a number of small townships inland were incorporated into the city. Here will be found a surprisingly large number of important buildings falling into the Modernisme category (see page 000), the Catalan equivalent of Art Nouveau. Avinguda de la Meridiana, coming from the north, exactly follows the line of the Greenwich meridian, while Avinguda del Paral.lel obtains its name from the fact that it runs parallel to the lines of latitude. The other main streets lie at angles of 45° to these; however, all street plans currently available show them as being exactly vertical or horizontal, which is not in accord with most other maps and can lead to confusion.

Pleasant, modern residential areas are to be found all round the city; industrial and trading sites are mainly in the north-east.

New Urbanism

Since it was decided that the 1992 Olympic Games would be held in Barcelona a hectic building programme has unfolded, which should help the city's infrastructure to cope with the heavy demands which will be placed upon it but will inevitably mean permanent changes in its appearance. Under the slogan "Barcelona, posa't Guapa" (Barcelona, make yourself beautiful), "Nou Urbanisme" is forging ahead everywhere, in an effort to solve the problems resulting from the existing inadequate structures. There is no doubt that a number of compromises will have to be made if the city is not to lose its existing atmosphere and charisma.

Infrastructural projects

The city is investing a lot of money and ambitious ideas in extending communications and tourist infrastructure. For example, some two dozen high-class hotels are being built; the airport at El Prat de Llobregat is being extended; the Estació de Franca (the railway station for France) is to be completely modernised; the Metro has seen extensions to lines, improvements to stations and new rolling stock; the remodelling of the Estació del Nord has provided the city with, for the first time, a central bus station for long distance services; the Catalonian National Theatre and Auditorium is being built on a former railway station site (adjoining Estació del Nord) on the Plaça de les Glòries Catalanes.

The port area, too, is profiting from modernisation; already complete is the Moll de la Fusta promenade, with restaurants, underground car park and subway. In the old harbour basin of Port Vell a shopping-centre with leisure and cultural facilities, as well as a water sports centre and all the necessary services are taking shape. A completely new venture is the Olympic Village further to the north-east, together with the Olympic Harbour and Convention Hall.

Moll de la Fusta, a new promenade

In the Montjuïc district not only is the Palau Nacional being completely modernised but the Botanical Gardens are being freshly laid out as well. A 260m/850ft radio tower is in course of erection on Montjuïc.

Population and Religion

The population of the city itself in 1989 was 1,707,286 (3,500,000 including the suburbs). This makes Barcelona Spain's largest city after Madrid.

The total is made up mainly of Catalans, together with some 760,000 Spaniards who have filtered in from other – mainly more backward – provinces and about 42,000 foreigners from various countries.

In 1900 Barcelona had 537,000 inhabitants; by 1930 the million mark was passed and in 1979 the figure reached 1,900,000. Since then the population has remained relatively constant, with a tendency to reduce slightly. The majority – 23.2% – fall into the fifteen to thirty age group.
There has been a clear trend towards leaving the city; during 1989 less than 5500 people moved into Barcelona from the surrounding province, while 16,000 turned their backs on it and moved out into the country.   Population growth

By far the majority of the population are Roman Catholics, the remainder being made up of Protestant, Muslim and Jewish minorities.   Religion

Administrative Districts

The city area of Barcelona, covering 99.09 sq.km/38¼ sq. miles, is divided up into ten districts, listed below in clockwise order, starting from the Old Town centre.   City

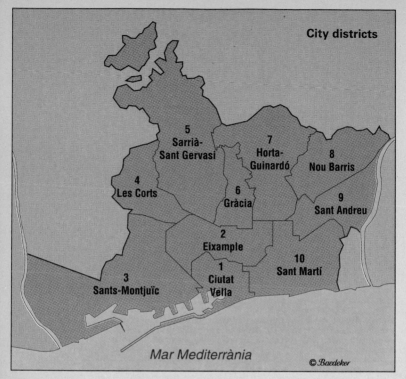

City districts

No.	Name	Inhabitants per sq.km	No. of inhabitants
1	Ciutat Vella	23,590	101,677
2	Eixample	39,429	287,948
3	Sants/Montjuïc	8853	184,772
4	Les Corts	15,102	91,004
5	Sarrià/Sant Gervasi	7722	154,523
6	Gràcia	3282	133,146
7	Horta/Guinardó	16,068	191,532
8	Nou Barris	24,505	196,046
9	Sant Andreu	22,578	147,664
10	Sant Martí	22,276	218,974
Barcelona total		17,230	1,707,286

Climate

General

Barcelona enjoys a fairly even Mediterranean climate, without excessive differences between minimum and maximum temperatures. The air temperature seldom falls below freezing point and hardly ever exceeds 35° C/ 95° F; during the day temperatures may fluctuate by between 6 and 15° C/ 11 and 27° F. The wind comes mainly from the south, and humidity is about

70% in the lower parts of the city, reducing as the land gets higher towards the coastal mountains. When there is little wind the atmosphere in the inner city can become heavily polluted by exhaust fumes and industrial gases.

Month	Approximate average temperature	Rainfall	Days of rain
January	10° C/50° F	5·6mm/0·2in	3
February	13° C/56° F	16·0mm/0.6in	6
March	13° C/56° F	31·2mm/1·2in	8
April	14° C/57° F	75·5mm/3·0in	13
May	18° C/65° F	19·9mm/0·8in	4
June	21° C/70° F	22·8mm/0·9in	7
July	25° C/78° F	2·9mm/0·1in	5
August	25° C/78° F	70·8mm/2·8in	8
September	22° C/72° F	53·3mm/2·1in	9
October	18° C/65° F	19·7mm/0·8in	4
November	16° C/61° F	113·7mm/4·5in	13
December	12° C/54° F	25·3mm/1·0in	8
Year	17.25° C/63.5° F	456·7mm/18·0 in	88

Culture

The city is an important educational centre. Pride of place must go to the University, which offers courses in biology, law, economic sciences, pharmacy, philology, philosophy, physics, geography and history, geology, mathematics, medicine, education, psychology and chemistry. The university buildings are widely scattered throughout the city and its immediate suburbs, with the greatest concentration being in the Zona Universitaria on the western edge of the city. At present some 58,000 students are registered.
There are branches of the University at Lleida (Lérida) and Tarragona.

The second important educational establishment is the Unniversidat Autònoma de Barcelona (Bellaterra; about 24,000 students), situated to the north-west of the city, in Sabadell and Cerdanyola. It specialises in economics and business management, information studies, politics and sociology, jurisprudence, philosophy, philology and medicine.

Most of the buildings of the Universitat Politècnica de Catalunya are also to be found mainly outside Barcelona, in Sabadell, Terrassa, Manresa, Vilanova i Geltru and Lleida. It specialises in architecture, agricultural science, civil engineering and road construction, telecommunications, information studies, nautical science, cybernetics, educational science, motor engineering, textile and energy technology, among others. At present it has about 15,000 students.

Law and economics are taught at the Universitat Pompeu Fabra, a private college.

These include the Catalonian Medical Academy, the Law Academy, the Academy of Fine Arts, the Pharmaceutical Academy and others.

In addition there are a number of training colleges, institutes offering correspondence courses and adult education centres.

Barcelona has two music colleges, the Municipal Conservatoire and the Liceu Conservatoire, an opera house. In addition there are schools teaching theatre, dance and choreography.

Language and Literature

Museums
The city boasts some fifty museums, some of world renown, such as the Museu d'Art de Catalunya (closed temporarily), the Museu Picasso and the Fundació Joan Miró. There are also a number of specialist museums, some of which are accessible only to qualified personnel. At the present time some museums are closed temporarily for renovation or remodelling, or offer viewing by prior arrangement only. For further details see A to Z section.

Libraries and archives
Pride of place goes to the University Library, with some 1,600,000 volumes if its specialist branches are included. Also of considerable importance, especially as far as books in the the Catalan dialect are concerned, is the Bibliotheca de Catalunya. In addition there are numerous local and children's libraries and those catering for specialist subjects as well as historical and scientific archives.

Publishing
Barcelona also enjoys a long and distinguished tradition in the world of publishing, founded on a determination – even during the Franco era – that Catalan literature would not be allowed to die. The city is the home of at least two hundred publishing houses, including some of Spain's most important book publishers. About a dozen daily newpapers are printed.

The annual "Liber" book fair is one of the most important events of its kind.

Music
Barcelona's musical tradition finds particular expression in two world-famous performance halls. The Palau de la Musica Catalana, also a building of considerable architectural merit in the Modernisme style, has its own chamber orchestra and also offers a wide spectrum of music ranging from classical to experimental, jazz, pop and rock.
The Liceu is the largest opera house in Spain, and in the whole of Europe only La Scala in Milan can better it. It maintains its own orchestra, and performances normally start in late autumn.
Mention should also be made of the fact that the soprano Montserrat Caballé and the tenor José Carreras, both world-famous singers, both hail from Barcelona.

Theatre
In conjunction with the present frantic rebuilding taking place in Barcelona in preparation for 1992, the National Theatre is going up near the Plaça de les Glòries Catalanes. Until it is opened theatrical performances are concentrated in some twenty five smaller theatres with varied repertoires.

Cultural sponsorship
The bigger banks and financial institutes, especially the Caixa de Barcelona and the Caixa de Pensions, are contributing a percentage of their profits to a large number of different cultural activities. For example, they are helping to maintain historically important buildings and finance museums and musical events.

Jocs Florals
A literary event with a long tradition is Barcelona's "Jocs Florals" (Flower Games), a poetry competition which has been held every year since 1859 with the aim of promoting Catalan literature.

Language and Literature

Official languages
As in the rest of Spain, Castilian (Castellano), or "high Spanish" is officially recognised as the prime language to be used in civil service and business circles in Catalonia. However, in Barcelona there has been a growing move for some years now to make Catalan the only language to be used officially; since 1975 it has become far more widely accepted in official circles and in schools, and has largely superceded Castilian. However, all Catalans are bi-lingual, and there is no need to learn Catalan specially for a holiday in Barcelona; a basic knowledge of Castilian will suffice, even though more and more road signs and other informative text may be only in Catalan.

However, anyone with a knowledge of French will soon master it, but making yourself understood verbally has its difficulties because of the rather strange accent the Catalans have.

Catalan, an original Romanesque language, displays considerable differences from pure Castilian and its vocabulary betrays a strong Provençal influence. In various dialect forms it is spoken by a total of some seven million people, in the Valencia region and in the Balearics as well as in Catalonia, and also in the foothills of the Pyrenees in eastern France, Andorra and even around the town of Alghero in Sardinia.
Unlike Castilian, Catalan lacks dipthongisation of the Latin root vowels (e.g. Latin portus, Castilian puerto, Catalan port; Latin bonus, Castilian bueno, Catalan bo). Final vowels disappear (e.g. Castilian dulce, Catalan dulc; Castilian muerte, Catalan mort). As well as the high Spanish verb forms ending in -ar, -er and -ir, Catalan has another form ending in -re (e.g. prendre, meaning "to take"). Examples of the Provençal influence on its vocabulary are words such as those for "table" (Castilian mesa, Catalan taula), "corn" (Castilian trigo, Catalan blat) or "window" (Castilian ventana, Catalan finestra).

Catalan

As in Portuguese, the unstressed a and e are almost swallowed, the unstressed o is short. The Castilian j as well as the g before e and i (pronounced like the Scottish ch in "loch" before a, o and u) become like the English j ("jug") in Catalan. Double L, roughly like ly in "badly" in Castilian, becomes more of a y in Catalan; where it is intended that it should be pronounced like a double l is in English the two letters are separated by a full stop or, occasionally, a hyphen. The Spanish letter ñ (pronounced roughly like ni in "onion") becomes ny, and Catalan knows no y as such; it is always written i. Ch is always hard, like k; nowadays c is nearly always used instead. The letter x always sounds like sh. The Castilian sound ch (like "chip") is replaced by tx, or often -ig at the end of a word. Z and c before e and i are not lisped as in Castilian, but are frequently pronounced more like an s. Catalan knows a double S (e.g., massa), whereas Castilian does not. The rules for stress correspond to those used in high Spanish, except that in the ending -ia there is no stress on the i (Castilian María, Catalan Maria). According to how the vowel is pronounced, emphasis may be by means of a grave (`) or acute (´) accent: an à always takes the grave, ú and í the acute; e and o take the grave when the vowel is open (e.g., cafè, arròs), and the acute when closed (consomé).

The Catalan accent

The first known examples of Catalan literature date from the 12th c. Historical works and chronicles cover a wide field, and there are numerous translations of the ancient classics and academic works from Moorish culture. On the other hand, original literary works are few and far between. The poetry and literary works of the Court troubadours from Provence, which flourished in the 12th and 13th c., had a considerable influence on Catalan authors, and many Provençal words and phrases found their way into the language. A central figure in Catalan language and culture was Ramon Llull (Raimundus Lullus in Latin). Born on the island of Mallorca, he lived from 1235–1316 and was a man of great education. Under him Catalan flourished as a cultural language to an extent it has not yet been able to match since. Lullus' essays, novels and poems, which have had such an important bearing on Western thinking, were written in his native idiom as well as in Latin and Arabic. As a result his works could be understood by the rank and file who understood only Catalan, as well as by the educated élite. He followed the idiom so closely that a Catalan can read his works today without any difficulty. Lullus' work "Libre de Cavalleria", the theme of which was how to lead the life of chivalry, was taken up by Joanot Martorell, who brought the Catalan romance of chivalry to its peak in his "Tirant lo Blanch" c. 1455. Mention should also be made here of the Valencian Arnau de Vilanova (c. 1240–1311), an equally learned and religious man.

Catalan literature

15

From the 15th c. onwards the Iberian Peninsula drew ever closer to Castille and the Castilian language; high Spanish is still known today as "castel-lano". As a result Catalan suffered a fate similar to that of the Provençal dialect which had filtered down from northern France, and with which it had so much in common; although it retained its importance as a spoken language it became supplanted by Castilian in the written word and, above all, in the literary sphere. In 1714, under a decree published by King Philip V, it was even banned from official use. This meant in practice that no original Catalan literature could be disseminated, and it was not until the Romantic period, with the re-awakening of past values and a realisation of its true importance, that Catalan was reborn. It was introduced into literary and intellectual circles, received support from sponsors and was the subject of detailed philological research. The linguist Maria Aguiló (1825–97) produced the first "Dictionary of Classical Catalan"; Tomás Forteza (1838–89) published a "Gramática Catalana", and Joan Alcover came up with the "Diccionari de la Llengua Catalana" prior to 1906.

The 19th c. literature concentrated on subjects from middle-class life. Particularly worthy of mention are Jacint Verdaguer i Santaló (1845–1902), a distinguished epic poet, still highly spoken of today, Emili Vilanova (1840–1905), humorist and comedy writer, and Pere Corominas (1870–1939), who wrote under the pen-name of Enrique Mercador, well known as a political and philosophical writer and as a freedom fighter in the Spanish Civil War.

When Spain was being regionalised and suffered from separatist uprisings during the late 1970s Catalan – which has been recognised once more as an official language since 1975 – enjoyed a further boost. Today there are Catalan books, periodicals and newspapers; the Third TV programme often broadcasts in the Catalan language; road signs and place-names have been changed; every bookshop has Catalan/Castilian dictionaries on sale – the list is endless. Recently scientific and academic books from abroad have been translated straight into Catalan, without first being put into Castilian. As a result of Catalan having been banned for so long in scientific circles it had inevitably failed to keep up with recent developments, so a whole new vocabulary covering modern terms had to be drawn up – in the same way that the Vatican was obliged to introduce new Latin words for such things as "data-processing", "atomic power" and "population explosion". There is one sphere that has remained unaffected by Franco's centralised cultural policy, that of local and regional history, where many historiographical works have been published solely in Catalan ever since the Renaixença.

However, as mentioned above, there is no need to worry about acquiring a knowledge of Catalan for your holiday. All mainland Catalans are bi-lingual, and most people working in tourist information offices, travel agents, hotels and restaurants and the larger shops speak English and/or French.

Customs and Traditions

As in most other large European towns and cities, old customs and traditions have tended to die away to a large degree, so we will dwell only on two key traditions which have survived and still play an important role in the lives of the people.

Sardana

The Sardana is a typically Catalan round dance in three-quarter or five-eighth time, with a mixture of short and long steps and quick and slow time, and is today often to be seen danced on the streets and squares of Barcelona, for instance, in front of the Cathedral or in Poble Espanyol. The music is based on popular tunes from the 16th and 17th c; instruments commonly used include flutes, oboes, trumpets, trombones, drums and double-bass.

Even though more and more criticism has been levelled in Spain of late at the bloody spectacle of the bullfight ("corrida de toros"), a visit to the arena is still one of the Spaniard's favourite leisure pursuits. Several pages in the newspapers are devoted to details of the fights and the toreros and the form of the animals. The visitor to Barcelona must make up his own mind whether he wishes to see a bullfight – he is bound to encounter one in some way or another.

Until the 16th c. bullfights were arranged in noble circles both as trials of strength and also at parties, the idea being that the caballero on horseback had to kill the bull with his lance. From the 17th c. onwards the fighting was done increasingly on foot; the rules used today are based largely on those drawn up by Francisco Romero, who was born about 1700 in Ronda.

In the round bullfighting arena the more expensive seats are on the shaded side ("sombra") and the cheaper ones on the sunny side ("sol"). The black and reddish brown beasts, which may not be more than six years old and weigh about 500kg/1100lbs, come mainly from Andalusian breeders.

The fight ("lidia") is made up of three main parts ("suertes"). After a short preliminary skirmish, in which the capeadores tease the bull with their brightly-coloured capes ("capa"), the mounted picadores commence the suerte de picar or suerte de varas, when they encourage the bull to attack them, pierce the enraged animal in the neck with their lances ("garrocha") and try to dull the force of its attack. When the bull is worn down ("castigado") by being speared by the lances ("varas") the second part of the show begins, the suerte de banderillas. The banderilleros approach the bull with several banderillas in their hands and, swerving away at the moment he attacks, pierce him in the neck. The banderillas normally used are sticks 75cm/30in long, with barbs and decorated with spangles; banderillas à cuerta are only 15cm/6in long. If the animals turn out to be too quiet or too insidious the men try to annoy them by making passes with their capes ("floreos"). When the beast has three pairs of banderillas in its neck the suerte suprema or suerte de matar begins. The espada or matador, equipped with scarlet cape ("muleta") and rapier ("estoque") begins by teasing the animal with the cape. Finally he tries to get it into a suitable position to deliver the final thrust ("estocada"). A punterillo administers the coup de grâce with a dagger in the neck of the beast which, if it had put up a brave and aggressive fight, would then be loudly clapped and cheered. Clumsy bullfighters are booed and whistled.

The bloody spectacle may be repeated six or eight times until darkness falls.

Economy and Transport

Economy

Barcelona is the main industrial centre in Catalonia and, together with Madrid, the most important in all Spain.

At the top of the list stands the metal industry, followed by textiles, machinery and automobile manufacture, structural and civil engineering and road construction, paper manufacture and printing. In 1989 there were some 12,500 industrial firms in existence, predominantly small and medium-sized undertakings.

Commerce far outweighs industry in Barcelona. In all there are some 37,000 firms operating in the spheres of wholesale (mainly textiles and leather goods, foodstuffs, technical equipment and road vehicles, furniture and household appliances) and retail trading (especially foodstuffs, textiles, shoes, chemical and pharmaceutical products, furniture, office supplies and printed items).

The Port of Barcelona

Services
The service sector has developed into one of enormous significance. There are some 25,000 firms involved, of which more than one-third are engaged in the hotel and restaurant trade, followed by transport, repair and servicing firms. Financial institutions and insurance companies also play a major rôle.

Transport

Public transport
The whole of the city is very well served by public transport. Most local travel is by underground on the Metro, with five lines covering almost all of Barcelona. This is supplemented by local lines of the Ferrocarrils de la Generalitat de Catalunya (FF.CC.), which serves the north-western outskirts and outlying areas, and also by trains belonging to RENFE, the Spanish state railway company, which run to the airport at El Prat de Llobregat, for example.
A complex network of bus routes and plenty of relatively cheap taxis mean that you can leave your own car behind if you wish when sightseeing in the city. In fact, such a course is to be recommended, because parking is very difficult indeed in the centre and unattended foreign vehicles are a target for thieves.
For more detailed information on public transport facilities in Barcelona see Practical Information, Transport.

Road network
The streets in the Old Town are mainly narrow and – like the wider boulevards in Eixample – many of them are one-way, making life difficult for anyone not familiar with the area. Road signs in the city are good and reliable.

Air travel
Barcelona airport is Spain's second largest after Madrid. It is about 12km/7½ miles south from the city centre, in the El Prat de Llobregat

district. In 1989 some 8,100,000 passengers were carried, and 61,000 tonnes of freight. The building of a new terminal by early 1992 is expected to increase the number of passengers to 12,000,000 per year.

For details see Practical Information, Air Travel.

The port (Port Franc de Barcelona) together with the outer harbour covers an area of about 300 hectares/750 acres. Once one of the major Mediterranean ports, it is still one of the most important in Spain. Port

In 1989 a total of 6555 ships unloaded here, a half of them from foreign ports. The total tonnage was 44·8 million gross register tonnes. In that year, too, the export turnover was 6,200,000 tonnes and the import figure 11,900,000 tonnes; 361,000 passengers came to Barcelona by sea, and passenger and ferry services, mainly for tourists, made an important contribution to the income of the Balearic Islands as well.

Famous People

Note

The following is an alphabetical list of important historical people who were born, lived, worked or died in Barcelona and made a reputation for themselves elsewhere in the world.

The Catalan family names are shown initially in full, but subsequently abbreviated to their more common form in the text (e.g., Ildefons Cerdà i Sunyer becomes Ildefons Cerdà).

Ildefons Cerdà i Sunyer (1815–76)

Nobody had a greater influence on the way Barcelona looks today than Ildefons Cerdà i Sunyer. After studying mathematics and architecture in Barcelona he went to Madrid in his twenties where he qualified as a roadworks engineer in 1841. His work as a civil servant took him to Tarragona and Girona and thence back to Barcelona, where he became deeply involved with town planning problems. In 1867 he published his "Teoria general de la urbanización" (General Theory of Town Planning), on the lines put forward by social Utopians. After fierce debate his plan for extending the city of Barcelona – taking due account of the social and infrastructural problems caused by the Industrial Revolution – was finally accepted in 1859 (see Barcelona from A to Z, Eixample).

His political career was just as important. As a member of the Progressive Party he was elected to the Cortes (the People's Parliament) in 1850 and in 1854 was made the city's legal adviser. The revolution of 1868, with the proclamation of a republic and the autonomous state of Catalonia, again put him in the political spotlight.

Ildefons Cerdà died in 1876 in Caldas de Besaya near Santander; in 1971 his mortal remains were taken to Barcelona and interred in the Cementiri Nou.

Josep Clarà i Ayats (1878–1958)

Josep Clarà i Ayats was born in Olot, in the Pyrenean foothills of Catalonia, and received most of his artistic education at the academy of art in Toulouse in France. In Paris, where he moved to in 1900, he met the French sculptors Aristide Maillol, Antione Bourdelle and Auguste Rodin, all of whom influenced his future work. Also of significance was his friendship with the American dancer Isadora Duncan; his most original and dynamic drawings date from this period.

Josep Clarà received recognition as an artist at a comparatively young age; his design for the memorial to the Catalonian Volunteers in the Parc de la Ciutadella in Barcelona won him the Grand Prize in Paris in 1925; in the same year he was made a member of the Academia de San Fernando, the Royal Academy of Art in Madrid. At the 1929 World Exhibition he received the only Medal of Honour awarded on that occasion. After a short stay in Greece he finally moved from Paris to Barcelona. On the suggestion of his sister Carmen his house in Barcelona was made into a museum in 1969, and a considerable number of his works are still on exhibition there.

Josep Comas i Solà (1868–1937)

Born in Barcelona, Josep Comas i Solà soon made his mark as an astronomer; he was only fifteen when he published an article in a French specialist magazine. After studying mathematics and physics he obtained a position in 1904 at the Fabra observatory, where he remained as head of its astronomical department until his death. In 1911 he also founded the Spanish-American Astronomical Society and published hundreds of articles on popular science in the Barcelona press. He discovered two comets, one of which was named after him, and eleven planetoids, of which the one numbered 945 and conspicuous because of the strong path it follows is called Barcelona.

Lluís Companys i Jover (1883–1940)

The politician and journalist Lluís Companys i Jover studied law at Barcelona University. He soon busied himself with political matters, founded the

Associació Escolar Republicana in 1900 and worked closely with the youth organisation known as Unió Federal Nacionalista Republicana. He became editor-in-chief of the autonomist newspaper "La Barricada", worked on "Publicidad" and was also a founder-member of the Republican Party of Catalonia in 1917, whose tract "La Lucha" he published. He became a fervent supporter of the workers' demands, which led to his being arrested together with some friends of similar persuasion in 1920 and imprisoned in Mahón castle on Minorca. During the military régime under General Primo de Rivera he again became active as a lawyer and joined the Catalan opposition parties. He was arrested again in October 1930, only to be elected leader of the Barcelona city council in April of the following year. It was while holding that post that shortly afterwards he proclaimed the Catalonian Republic. Following the death of Francesc Macià in 1933 he took office as president of the Generalitat. When General Franco's troops entered Barcelona in 1939 he sought exile in France, was taken prisoner there by German troops and brought back to Spain. His strong involvement with the Catalonian Left led to his being court-martialled, and on 15 October 1940 he was shot in the fortress on Montjuïc.

The theologian and writer Miquel Costa i Llobera came from an aristocratic Majorcan family. During his student days in Barcelona he came into contact with Jacint Verdaguer, among others. His first works were published in 1873 in "Revista Balear", and the poem "El pi de Formentor" – still recognised as a masterpiece of Catalan poetry – caused quite a sensation in 1875. Technically speaking, most of his work was on ancient Classical lines; his influence on the Catalan language and its poetry is still felt today.

Miquel Costa i Llobera (1854–1922)

Born in Barcelona, Lluis Domènach i Montaner was one of the architects who helped Modernisme in Barcelona to unfold in the unique way it did. After studying architecture in Barcelona and Madrid he received a professorship at the College of Architecture in his native city. The approach of the 1888 World Exhibition led to a flurry of building activity, and he seized the opportunity to submit his first important designs. Three times he received the prize awarded by the city of Barcelona for the finest building of the year, and three times he was elected president of the Ateneu, Barcelona's most important cultural body at the time. The thread running through his published writings was his strong allegiance to the cause of Catalan nationalism.

Lluis Domènach i Montaner (1850–1923)

The most outstanding Barcelona building which he designed is the Palau de la Música Catalana, closely followed by the Hospital de la Santa Creu i de Sant Pau.

Antoni Gaudí, born in Reus in the province of Tarragona, is by far the most important Spanish architect of recent times. He was trained at the College of Architecture in Barcelona, at a time when Historicism and the Neo-Gothic were the very quintessence of all building. Gaudí was strongly drawn to Gothic, even though he strongly criticised some of its technical details, such as the use of buttresses, which he regarded as little more than crutches and wished to see replaced by sloping supports. His ideal was the reintroduction of a light, colourful Mediterranean form of Gothic, and such Gothic elements do in fact dominate many of his buildings. However, his very own creative design embraced the combining of historical patterns with plant forms woven in the Art Nouveau style, leading to the style known as Modernisme (see page 34), which also made itself felt in the literary sphere.

Antoni Gaudí (1852–1926)

Gaudí's principal works are found in Barcelona, where he built private residences, such as Casa Milà, Casa Batilò, and churches which on the one hand reflect Gothic forms, and on the other display a striking similarity to the designs of a Rudolf Steiner.

Gaudí received generous support and encouragement from the aristocratic industrialist Eusebi Güell, who asked him to design him a residence, the Palau Güell near the Ramblas, a country seat, Finca Güell and a housing

Antoni Gaudí

Joan Miró

Charlie Rivel

estate for his workers, the Colonia Güell in Santa Coloma del Cervelló to the south-west. Gaudí's best-known building, however, is the Temple de la Sagrada Família in the north of the city; he devoted most of his working life to it, but this "Church of the Poor", as he called it, remains unfinished to this day.

Antoni Gaudí died as the result of a tram accident. Unrecognised, he was first taken to a hospital for the poor, and his true identity was only discovered just before he died.

Eusebi Güell i Bacigalupi (1846–1918)

It is impossible to imagine that architecture would have developed the way it did during the Modernisme period without Eusebi Güell i Bacigalupi, the extremely successful industrialist who was the great friend and patron of the architect Antonio Gaudí. After having studied political science, law and natural science in France and Great Britain as well as Spain, he founded the first Portland cement factory in Catalonia, ran a railway company and a bank and went in for viniculture. Active, too, in the political field, he became a member of parliament for the province, a city councillor and senator. In 1900 he chaired the Jocs Floral de Barcelona, the poetry competition which had been set up in 1859 and is held every year. His house on the Carrer Nou de la Rambla, now the Theatrical Museum, was a mecca for well-known writers, painters, musicians and other aesthetes of the period. In 1918 he was elevated to the peerage.

Christopher Columbus (1451–1506)

For years a number of Mediterranean towns laid claim to having been the birthplace of the discoverer of America, but recent researches have established beyond doubt that he was born in Genoa. However, the exact date of birth of Christopher Columbus (Cristofol Colom in Catalan) is not known, but it was between 25 August and 31 October 1451. He became involved with seafaring and marine trade at an early age and came to Lisbon in Portugal in 1476, where he looked into the possibilities of finding the sea-route to India, the existence of which had been known since ancient times, but the king showed no interest. On his way to France he passed through Spain where, in the monastery of La Rábida, the father-confessor of the Spanish Queen Isabella gave him a letter of introduction to her. She agreed a contract with him for the voyage of discovery, and bestowed on him the ranks of Grand Admiral and Viceroy of the region he hoped to discover. In addition he was to receive one-tenth of the anticipated profit from the venture.

On August 3rd 1492 the tiny fleet, made up of the caravels "Santa Maria", "Pinta" and "Niña", set sail on a westerly course from the port of Palos de la Frontera on the Atlantic southern coast of Spain, hoping to find India. For three long weeks the sailors saw nothing but sky and sea, and hopes of finding land grew dimmer and dimmer. The crew became restless, but after Columbus had altered course to south-west an island came into view, which he, on first setting foot on it, named San Salvador, although more than likely it was in fact Watling Island in the Bermudas. On the same voyage Columbus also reached Cuba and Haiti, where he left behind a group of 39 volunteers. He then returned to Spain in order to bring news of his success in person to the King and Queen. In all he made three more journeys westward, without any real plaudits or financial gain being put his way in Spain; people were disillusioned by the fact that – instead of the legendary rich land of India being discovered – he had found only what they regarded as a rough, uncultured land inhabited by savages and with no real economic prospects. The crews who sailed with him also took it into their heads to denounce him and make things very difficult for him, even to the extent that, on his third voyage to Hispaniola (Haiti), he was seized and brought back to Spain in chains. However, he successfully defended himself before the king and queen and was rehabilitated. Nevertheless he never really received the honour his success warranted; even the New World which he discovered was named not after him but after a less important rival, the Italian Amerigo Vespucci.

At the 1888 World Exhibition the Columbus Memorial was erected in Barcelona harbour, with his statue on the top of it. However, it faces the sea, not in the opposite direction towards America.

The Frenchman Ferdinand de Lesseps, who built the Suez Canal, was his country's consul in Barcelona from 1842–48. People have not forgotten the way he came to the assistance of the city during the 1842 bombardment in which General Joaquin Alvarez Espartero suppressed a people's revolt. The uprising had come about as a result of a planned trade agreement with England which would have seriously hindered the industrialisation of Catalonia which was just beginning to take shape.

Ferdinand de Lesseps (1805–94)

Born the son of an industrialist, Joan Maragall i Gorina, although a qualified lawyer, is best remembered as a writer. In 1890 he joined the editorial staff of the "Diario de Barcelona"; a year later his first poems and translations were published. Being financially independent he was able to devote himself to his literary ambitions, and his work as a journalist helped pave the way to Modernisme.
As a translator Joan Maragall was instrumental in introducing the works of such people as Goethe and Nietzsche to Spain.

Joan Maragall i Gorina (1860–1911)

Born in Portbou, on the Franco-Spanish border, the sculptor and art-collector Frederic Marès i Deulovol established one of Barcelona's most interesting museums. His travels took him to Brussels, Paris, Florence and Rome, and from 1946–64 he was the director of the Academy of Art in Barcelona. He has been responsible for the construction of a number of memorials.

Joan Maragall i Gorina (1860–1911)

Born in Montroig near Barcelona the artist Joan Miró was first inspired by the French Realists and, above all, by Cubism which was then just coming into its own and which he encountered in Paris on his first visit there in 1919. A little later he was one of the signatories of the Surrealist Manifesto; in 1923 he turned away from traditional painting and from Cubism and developed his own characteristic style. Miró's compositions display powerful and bold lines together with strong colours, with no suggestion of the abstract, and arouse many objective associations in the mind. He also worked with etching and printing techniques as well as in ceramics and sculpture. Until 1940 he lived mainly in Paris, but then fled back to neutral Spain when the Germans invaded the French capital. When Paris was liberated by the Allies in 1944 Miró was able to return to France. After the end of the war he moved to the island of Mallorca, where he died on Christmas Day 1983.

Joan Miró (1893–1983)

The Fundació Joan Miró on Montjuïc displays a most comprehensive collection of this artist's works.

Josep Pla I Casadevall (b. 1897)

Josep Pla i Casadevall came from the Baix Empordà region, and after studying law turned to journalism, initially with provincial publications. As foreign correspondent on various daily newspapers he went to France, Italy, Germany and the Soviet Union during the years 1919–39. It was during this period, too, that he published his first literary efforts, in the form of short stories, reports on his travels, biographies, etc. During the Spanish Civil War he lived mainly abroad, but returned to Catalonia in 1939. Although until then he had written mainly in Castilian, from 1945 onwards he turned completely to his native Catalan tongue, leavening the dialect and idioms of the region with plenty of his own linguistic imagination and vividness of expression.

Josep Puig i Cadafalch (1867–1957)

Josep Puig i Cadafalch from Matató was the third great architect of the Catalonian Modernisme movement. Like Antoni Gaudí, he gained much of his inspiration from Gothic architecture, enriching it with local characteristics and much decoration. He was responsible in particular for a number of purpose-built industrial buildings, mainly for the 1929 World Exhibition, as well as collaborating in building on the Plaça de Catalunya and Via Laietana and in the archaeological digs which uncovered the ancient site at Empúries. He lectured at the Sourbonne in Paris and at Harvard University in the U.S.A., and for a time worked on the Catalan newspapers "La Renaixença" and "La Veu de Catalunya". From the turn of the century he also influenced the region's educational policy.

Charlie Rivel (José Andreo Rivel; 1896–1983)

Born in Cubellas near Barcelona, the son of a family of Spanish artistes, Charlie Rivel , the "acrobat schöön", entranced circus audiences all his life. He was one of the "silent" clowns, whose jokes are never coarse and who amuse their audiences while awakening in them a feeling of melancholy and sympathy as a result of the tragic adversities which cause the clown all sorts of unhappiness, the like of which is only too familiar to us all. Charlie Rivel, whose hallmarks were an almost square red nose and a long, narrow pullover which came down below his knees, had the gift of making himself understood by those watching him without ever saying a word. He was a virtuoso of the onomatopoeic sounds with which he accompanied his act. A bronze statue to this world-famous artiste stands in the leisure park on Montjuïc.

Josep Lluís Sert i López (b. 1902)

The architect Josep Lluis Sert i López is one of the leading men in his profession in Catalonia. He was strongly influenced by working with Le Corbusier in Paris in 1929–30 and also by the Bauhaus school of architectural design. The founding, with his support, of the GATCPAC (Grup d'Arquitectes i Tècnics Catalans per al Progrés de l'Arquitectura Contemporània) in 1930 formed part of the same line of thought. In 1937 he designed the Spanish Pavilion for the Paris World Exhibition; since 1945 he has drawn up plans for a number of South American cities. In 1953 he succeeded Walter Gropius as head of the Faculty of Architectural Studies at Harvard University, and ran his own architect's office in Cambridge, Illinois, with considerable success. Since 1955 he has established strong contacts in Europe again; the Fondation Maeght in St-Paul-de-Vence, in southern France, and the Fundació Miró om Montjuïc have been set up.

Antoni Tàpies (b. 1923)

A native of Barcelona, Antoni Tàpies is one of the most important artists of the present day. His early works were strongly influenced by the Surrealists, especially Joan Miró, a personal friend. At the start of the fifties Tàpies went to Paris and mastered the newly arrived Tachismus style of painting (from the French word "tache", meaning spot or fleck, thus painting by flicking the colour on to the canvas), a variation from the more formal method, which led from Surrealism to total Abstraction. His subjects – he frequently works more with coloured plaster, ceramics and other materials more akin to sculpting than painting – portray a most unfamiliar language of symbols and signs. Tàpies has also made a name for himself as a draughtsman and illustrator.

Periodic special exhibitions by the Fundació Antoni Tàpies display a selection from his many works.

Like Miquel Costa i Llobera, a close friend, Jacint Verdaguer i Santaló was both poet and churchman. As chaplain of the "Companyia Transatlàntica" he crossed the Atlantic nine times in less than two years; his epic poem "L'Atàntida" became known throughout the world. His most successful years were those spent serving in the household of the Marques de Comillas de Barcelona, the owner of the shipping line. In 1884 he went on a "Grand Tour", taking him to France, Germany and Russia, and in 1886 he visited the Holy Land.

Jacint Verdaguer i Santaló (1845–1902)

At the age of forty he took stock of himself and decided to change his life completely and renounce his duty of obedience to the church. Such a radical change found favour neither with the Count of Comillas nor with the church hierarchy, and he was prohibited from saying mass. What had happened led to much public murmuring and he was reinstated in 1898. Jacinct Verdaguer counts among the most popular of Catalan writers of epic poetry, perhaps his most important work being his description of the customs, myths and legends of his homeland.

History of Barcelona

c. 130,000 B.C.	Back in the Interglacial Period there are human settlements in what is now Catalonia, especially near the River Ter.
5th c. B.C.	Man progresses from hunting animals and gathering food to cultivating fields and rearing cattle. Main settlements are in the Llobregat valley.
2nd c. B.C.	Man learns to plough with a yoke.
	Early records indicate that there are Iberians on the eastern coast of Spain. Some researchers believe them to be the predecessors of the Basques and probably related to the Berbers of North Africa.
c. 2000 B.C.	First traces of Iberian occupation, especially near the later settlement of Barcino.
1st c. B.C.	Catalonian urn-field culture.
6th c. B.C.	Celts come over the Pyrenees to Catalonia and a Celto-Iberian mixed culture develops. Some of the ports along the east coast of Spain, including Emporion (now Empúries or Ampurias) are colonised by Greeks, mainly Ionians from the Phocaean colony of Massalie (Marseilles).
After 6th c. B.C.	The Carthaginians begin to drive out the Greeks.
236–203 B.C.	After the First Punic War the Carthaginians extend their colonial power northward to the Ebro; present-day Catalonia remains under the influence of the Roman Empire.
218 B.C.	Barcino said to be founded by the Carthaginian general Hamilkar Barkas (but in fact he died in 229 B.C.).
201 B.C.	Under a peace treaty with Rome Carthage gives up its Spanish possessions. A little later (197 B.C.) Rome establishes the provinces of Hispanio Citerior, capital Tarraco (Tarragona), and Hispania Ulterior (now Andalusia). A series of risings by the Celts (143–133 B.C.) hampers the complete subjection of the peninsula but not the rapid linguistic and cultural Romanisation of the country.
81–72 B.C.	The Roman praetor Sertorius, a supporter of Marius, tries to establish an independent Celti-iberian state.
27 B.C.	Spain is divided into the provinces of Hispania Tarraconensis (in the northeast, around the present town of Tarragona), Hispania Lusitania (in the west, between Duero/Douro and Guadiana) and Hispania Baetica (the original Hispania Ulterior).
19 B.C.	The Iberian peninsula is fully incorporated into the Roman Empire by Augustus.
At about the time of the birth of Christ	Since the time of the Emperor Augustus (63 B.C.–A.D. 14) Barcelona has been a Roman colony under the name of Colonia Julia Augusta Faventia Paterna Barcino.
After A.D. 100	Beginning of the Christianisation of the Iberian peninsula.
A.D. 414	The Visigoths (West Goths) under King Athaulf advance into Catalonia (Gotalonia) and make Barcinona their capital.

King Eurich, ruler of the Visigothic kingdom of Tolosa, defeats the Suevi and establishes Visigothic rule throughout Spain (except the north-west).	466–484
The conversion of the Arian Visigoths to orthodox Catholicism is followed by their rapid amalgamation with the Romanised population.	587
The Moors take the city and name it Bardschaluna.	716
Charlemagne founds the Spanish March as a defensive outpost against the Moorish caliphate of Córdoba; Louis the Good conquers Barcelona in 801 and makes it the capital of the March. Catalonia is linked with the south of France by the Strata Francisca.	778
Wifred of Barcelona founds the independent province of Catalonia. A Catalan "nationalist feeling" begins to unfold, and freedom from the French yoke begins.	874
Almansor ("the Victorious"), grand vizier of Caliph Hisham II, conquers Barcelona – the farthest expansion of Moorish military power in Spain.	985
Barcelona is the capital of a state which is once more independent.	988
The Counts of Barcelona, Urgell and Besalú and the Bishops of Barcelona, Girona, Vic and Eine take up arms together against the Caliphs of Córdoba.	1010
Under the joint rule of the brothers Berenguer Ramon I (1018–35) and Ramon Berenguer I (1035–76) the region of the province of Barcelona is enlarged.	1018–76
The marriage of Ramon Berenguers IV and an Aragonese princess unites Catalonia and Aragón.	1137
Alfonso I of Barcelona (Alfonso II of Aragón) extents Catalonia's domain as far as the French regions of Béarn, Bigorre, Carcassonne, Béziers and Nîmes.	1162–96
In the Cathar Wars the French lose many of their possessions in Catalonia. Barcelona begins to expand beyond the Roman walls.	1209–29
Jaime I ("the Conqueror") seeks political expansion in the Mediterranean region. In 1229 he leads a successful punitive expedition against the Majorcan pirates and fights his way into Palma.	1213–76
Pedro III ("the Great") annexes Sicily, which remains part of the House of Barcelona until the 15th c. Royal shipyards (Reales Atarazanas) built in Barcelona.	1276–85
The Cortes (permanent representatives of the Church, the secular nobility and the towns and cities) of Aragón, Catalonia and Valencia act in unison.	After 1307
The marriage of Fernando II of Aragón and Isabella of Castille leads to unification of the former rival kingdoms. The rule of the Reyes Católicos (Catholic Kings) leads to a transition to an Absolute Monarchy. As a result, a strong sense of self-awareness among the Catalonians results in uprisings against the Throne, especially in the 15th and 17th c.	1469
The conquest of Granada ends the Reconquista, the re-conquering of Spain by Christians. Isabella supports Christopher Columbus, whose voyages of discovery and exploration prepare the way for the establishment of the Spanish colonial empire in America.	1492
Charles I, a Habsburg, becomes king of Castile and Aragón. After the death of his grandfather Maximilian I he inherits the Habsburg territories in 1519, as Charles V (coronation in Rome 1530), he becomes Holy Roman Emperor.	1516

History of Barcelona

1571	In the naval battle of Lepanto (Greek name Naupaktos) at the entrance to the Gulf of Corinth the Turkish fleet is annihilated by Spanish warships, assisted by those of Venice and the Holy See. Commander of the Spanish fleet is Don Juan d'Austria, a half-brother of Philip II. This naval victory ensures Spain's dominance of the Mediterranean.
1640	The increased tax burden leads to uprisings against the Crown in Catalonia, which are not finally crushed until 1652.
1659	The Peace of the Pyrenees sees the end of Spain's war with France which had lasted since 1635. Under the treaty Spain cedes Roussillon and Cerdagne to France, resulting in a split in the Catalan cultural sphere on either side of the Pyrenean chain.
1714	Philip V removes all the special rights formerly enjoyed by the Catalonians. The Catalan language is forbidden in official circles.
1778	The abolition by Charles III of the Castilian monopoly on overseas trade bodes well for the future economic development of Catalonia.
1834	Introduction of a moderately liberal constitution.
1834–39	First Carlist War. Don Carlos, Ferdinand VII's brother, declares himself king (Charles V) in opposition to the regency of the Queen Mother, Maria Cristina of Naples, during the minority of Isabella II. He is supported by the Basque provinces as well as Aragón and Catalonia, but the enterprise fails and he is forced to flee to France in 1839.
1847–39	The first workers' guilds and consumer co-operatives are formed in Barcelona.
1847–49	The Second Carlist Wars and republican risings aggravate internal conflicts.
1859	After animated discussions the plan by the building engineer Ildefons Cerdá for extending the built-up area of the city is accepted. As a result

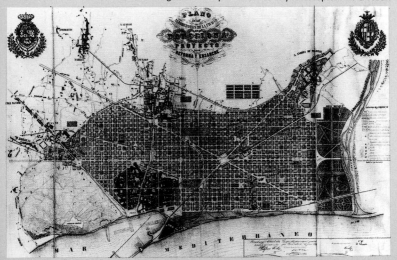

Original sketch by Ildefons Cerdá for the new district of Eixample

the Eixample – that extensive part of the city with buildings largely in the Modernisme style which stretches from the Old Town to the foot of the coastal mountains – takes shape in the years that follow.

September Revolution. Isabella II is deposed and goes into exile. First Spanish Republic.   1868

The Third Carlist War, initiated by Don Carlos' grandson, is directed against King Amadeo I, a son of Victor Emmanuel II of Italy and against the First Republic proclaimed by the Cortes in 1873. Mass socialist risings in the city and surroundings.   1872–76

World Exhibition held in Barcelona, resulting in an extensive new building project concentrating on the new Modernisme style.   1888

Autonomist movements in Catalonia, the Basque country and Galicia.   After 1890

The first congress promoting the use of the Catalan language is held in Barcelona. One of its main aims is standardisation of Catalan which – since Philip V revoked all Catalonia's special privileges in 1714 – has existed only as a spoken language.   1906

The founding of the Institut d'Estudis Catalans (Institute of Catalan Studies) indicates the growing importance of the Catalan language, which is gradually becoming accepted in official quarters.   1907

Following the agreement in 1904 between Spain and France on spheres of influence in North Africa, Spanish campaigns against Morocco lead to strong protests. The Barcelona General Strike ("Semana Tragica") is put down with much bloodshed.   1909

Founding of the Catalonian Mancomunitat (self-government with the emphasis on cultural autonomy). Self-government is disbanded again in 1925.   1914

Spain remains neutral in the First World War.   1914–18

General Primo de Rivera establishes a military dictatorship, with Alfonso XIII's approval. Dissolution of the Cortes.   1923

A further World Exhibition is held in Barcelona.   1929

After a Republican victory in the local government elections Alfonso XIII leaves the country. Beginning of the Second Republic. The Progressive-Liberal constitution provides inter alia for the regional autonomy of Catalonia, which becomes law in 1932. The Catalan language is permitted in offices and schools, and an increasing number of newpapers and books appear in Catalan.   1931

The Spanish Civil War breaks out following the murder of the Monarchist member of parliament Calvo Sotelo and the military rising led by General Francisco Franco y Bahamonde in Spanish Morocco. Franco and other generals set up a rival government in Burgos.   1936–39

Franco's troops occupy Catalonia. The Franco dictatorship revokes the autonomy granted to the Catalans in 1932.   1939

During the Second World War Spain remains neutral in spite of its links with the Berlin-Rome axis.   1939–45

Lluis Companys, President of the Generalitat, is shot in Montjuïc fortress.   1940

A national referendum approves Franco's plan to restore the monarchy at a later date.   1947

History of Barcelona

1966	The monastery on Montserrat publishes a religious monthly tract "Serra d'Or", the first publication in the Catalan language since 1939.
1972–73	Strikes in Catalonia.
1975	On Franco's death Prince Juan Carlos becomes King Juan Carlos I of Spain. Catalan, Basque and Galician are recognised as teaching and official languages.
1978	After a plebiscite a new democratic constitution comes into force; Spain becomes a constitutional monarchy.
1979	In a referendum Catalans decide on far-reaching self-government for the region. In November the Spanish Lower House grants by a majority decision a Statute of Autonomy.
1980	In Catalonia a regional parliament is elected. Other regions also seek a statute of autonomy.
1986	Spain joins the EC. Serious forest and plain-fires destroy most of the plant life and trees in the Eastern Pyrenees and on Montserrat. On 17 October Barcelona is nominated to host the 1992 Olympic Games.
1987	On 19 June the militant Basque separatist organisation ETA sets off a bomb in a department store in Barcelona, killing fifteen and injuring many more.
1988	With the arrival of the Olympic Flag from Seoul (South Korea) on 9 October the Cultural Olympics are officially opened in anticipation of 1992. Queen Elizabeth II visits the Olympic site on Montjuïc.
1992	Simultaneously with the XXV Summer Olympics in Barcelona, 1992 will also be celebrated throughout the country as the quincentenary of the discovery of America by Christopher Columbus, and numerous events and cultural activities are planned.

Barcelona in Quotations

BARCELONA AT DIFFERENT TIMES OF DAY (1958)

Wolfgang
Koeppen
German author
(b. 1906)

The Ramblas, the streets which lead from the harbour to the city centre, are narrow, old and friendly. A tree-lined avenue runs down the middle with chairs scattered about where you can sit and dream, and immediately you know that this is an ancient city-state, a polis. Men stand around in conversation and sit arguing under the trees. Their gestures are expressive and yet have a certain dignity. This one could be Demosthenes, that one Kleon, the tanner. This is how political parties were once formed and tyrants toppled. But their conversation is not concerned with politics; waving a rolled-up cycling newspaper they are discussing the football results. The policemen, armed with machine guns, guarding the main entrance to the police station, sit enjoying the shade like the cat among the mice next to them . . .

At this hour of the day the houses are like cool fortresses protected against the sun. The darkened rooms are cosy and pleasant. Perhaps Pan with his magical shepherd's crook and the ancient wisdom of leisure has crossed the Mediterranean. But at five o'clock Mercury awakes. The streets come to life. The bells of the old tramcars ring. Cars rattle by. The newspaper vendors raise their loud voices. The siesta is over and like everywhere else they try to cheat the customer . . .

Among the confusion of these narrow streets (Barri Gòtic – Ed.) stands the Cathedral. It seems more Moorish than Gothic. The visitor is guided by colonnades to a palm courtyard. The palm trees are so close together that their crowns touch each other forming a shady roof like that of a dense primeval forest. There is a pond beneath and behind a decorative wrought-iron grille white geese stretch their necks like stupidly arrogant guardians. The nave is as gloomy as the bottom of the sea. The Cathedral is a former mosque. Its columns are like stone palm trees which intertwine to form the roof, casting its heavy shadow over the choir and altar, over the worshippers in communion and the priests in their vestments. Everything is enveloped by the dark shadows and each candle creates its own little glow in the mountain of darkness . . .

What else is there to see? The church of the Sagrada Família by Antonio Gaudí, a Barcelona architect, who even after his death is considered to be more progressive than Le Corbusier. His cathedral is built in the style of an Expressionist sugar baker, a fairytale tower for worshippers and much more friendly than the other churches in the city. Gaudí must have been a jovial man. He has built a house in a main street in the form of waves with the inhabitants looking out of the windows like despairing swimmers.

SPANISH JOURNEY (1910)

Julius Meier-
Graefe
German author
(1867–1935)

Around midnight we went down to the folk festival in Güell Park. The word "park" sounds harmonious and peaceful. It conjures up images of quiet avenues with graceful women and babies dressed in white, even green trees. In Güell Park you can forget these ideas. I don't know whether the name Güell sounds more attractive in Spanish than it does to North European ears. Utrillo's idea to take us to the park at midnight when bourgeois people like us have usually been in bed for ages was in itself suspicious. And especially in Güell Park. The last syllable contradicted everything that was suggested by the first. I couldn't help imagining something bizarre. This was unfortunate for I believe that without being prepared at all, it could be a great shock in the middle of the night . . .

Finally, it must have been two o'clock, we reached a sort of cave or rather a temple or a giant carousel which was stationary. It was supported by columns which ressembled elephant teeth or whalebones. From there a path bordered by steep slopes that were littered with skulls or whatever, led to a plateau that on closer inspection turned out to be a hanging garden and was the roof of the temple in which we had been earlier. Then we came to a flower bed, which was a kilometre wide and closely-packed with people instead of flowers. Next to it was another flower bed, and so on. I don't know how many. The monstrous things seemed to hover in the air and the people in them were unaware of the danger. In any case we had not enough time to think about it, for in a flash we faced another incredibly shaped building, half Indian Palace, half dog-kennel, made from faience or glass or soap bubbles. Utrillo told us calmly about Catalonia, as if we were sitting together quite normally. I pulled myself together, remained still and eagerly took in the closest details of a spittoon or monument. It was real faience and in the shapes I easily recognised traits of Horta and Guimard (well known Art Nouveau architects – Ed.). The memory of a house (Casa Mià – Ed.) which I had seen days before in the Gracia came to my aid. I was not in a trance but in modern architecture. Oh, how I regretted all I had thought against Horta and Guimard, Endell and Obrist and whatever else the miscreants are called. Besides the ideas of this monster they all seemed like peaceful classicists. Utrillo explained that this man was going to build a cathedral and had many commissions. Barcelona was divided into two parties, those against him, those for him. He was a man of great energy and he still had a long way to go.

Wolfgang Weber   BARCELONA (1928)
German journalist

With an almost irrational sense of liberality, which in other countries would long since have been inhibited by calculation and deliberation, the unheard of is performed daily in Barcelona. And it is this very irrationality and daring which gives the town the mark of the unusual. Or is it not of unparalleled audacity for a strict Catholic country to recklessly build a road through the palaces and churches of the Old Town to the harbour? And it is far-sighted, almost beyond our comprehension, to be already building the underground below a new suburban road, where there are no houses, but where it will one day be needed.

How does Barcelona evolve? For example: when a new road is being built in the inner city they continue building it at its full width out into the unpopulated countryside. Right up to the point where the fields begin it is immaculately concreted and provided with tram lines and carefully nurtured plane trees. And on this road a house is built, a palace with ten storeys, a dozen shops on the ground floor and all modern conveniences. A house and a road – that should be sufficient impetus to carry on building, to tempt the inhabitants of the dirty city, and at the same time to contribute to the outskirts looking the same as the inner city. "In the beginning the road" – Californian law on European soil!

In the inner city – the same largesse. The new town is strictly divided up into square blocks, not by narrow streets as in America, but by 60 metre wide avenues of plane trees.

The gigantic Plaza Cataluña arose through the demolition of an entire residential quarter and was excavated to form the underground railway station. The fire-damaged harbour district of Barceloneta was not salvaged but torn down and rebuilt at the city's expense. Barcelona is one of the few cities of the world that has an underground system; tram cars with electric doors; twice as many cars as the entire Hamburg area; and is building two new concourses onto the old one of a railway station, although there are only nine trains a day. Everything is larger than life, everywhere one expects developments to exceed those which have gone before.

IMPRESSIONS FROM SPAIN (1866)

Hans Christian
Andersen
Danish writer
(1805–75)

I ambled further and ended up in a street which was even narrower and more crowded than the one I had come from. I shall call it the street of churchgoers. Here, squeezed in between high houses is Barcelona's cathedral which is so unimpressive and lacking in greatness that you can pass by it without even noticing it. It is the same as with many famous personalities: someone actually has to touch you on the arm and point them out to you. The crowd jostled me on the arm and I was pushed through the small door into the open arcade, which adjoins the church with a row of altars and encloses a courtyard of orange trees, planted at a time when a mosque stood here. The waters of the great marble basin where the Moors used to wash their faces before and after prayers still splashed. In the centre of it stood a pretty small bronze statuette of a rider on horseback with water spurting up around it. Closeby goldfish swam among luxuriant water plants and behind the grille geese were swimming, I would rather have said swans but one must keep to the truth if one wants to be an original travel writer. Riders in fountains and live geese were not conducive to worship and yet although there was so much else here the atmosphere was dominated by the ecclesiastical. Before the altars of the arcade people knelt in worship and incense streamed from the large open doorway of the church with organ and choirs resounding. I entered. Underneath the mighty arches there was a sense of gravity and greatness, yet God's sunlight could not penetrate the painted windows. The brooding half-darkness made denser by the incense was too oppressive for my thoughts of God. I longed for the open courtyard, whose ceiling is the sky, where the sunbeams fall between orange trees and rippling water. It was outside where the pious knelt, that the full gentle sounds carried my thoughts upwards to God and I first experienced divine worship in Spain.

I left the church and came through the narrow street into another that was equally narrow, yet shining with gold and silver. In Barcelona and several other Spanish cities things have not changed since the Middle Ages with the various craft guilds, for example, the shoemakers and the metal workers each having their own street where they sell their wares so that the whole range is on display. I found myself in the street of the goldsmiths. Here, one shop after another was full of gold chains and beautiful jewellery.

Modernisme

Barcelona is the very hub of Modernisme, a typically Catalan art style which dominated architecture and arts and crafts in particular, but literature, music and dancing as well at the end of the 19th and early 20th c.; simply to call it the "Catalan Art Nouveau" would be a rather inadequate way of describing it although the two are, broadly speaking, contemporary.

The origins of Modernisme are to be found in the Renaixença, or Renaissance, when Catalonia began to think back on its history and its own language and culture. A simultaneous sudden growth of Barcelona's urban area and the number of its inhabitants in a period of industrial and economic prosperity produced a well-to-do middle-class of people and provided money for extensive building programmes and city planning, all factors whch combined to foster a sense of self-esteem spreading far beyond the city and its environs. People longed to be able to compete with the greatest cities in Europe, and the 1888 World Exhibition in Barcelona meant that the eyes of the world were upon it. Thus Modernisme evolved as an upper-class cultural form developing in tandem with the sense of national pride and awareness then being experienced by the Catalan people as a whole.

The Modernisme form was based primarily on Impressionism, while also incorporating a richly varied amalgam of Historicism and Art Nouveau. The latter were quite clearly divorced in some other parts of Europe, but in Modernisme – especially in the works of the architect Antoni Gaudí – they were often combined in the same subject, with varying degrees of emphasis. The Eixample, that expansion of the city funded largely by the upper classes in the 19th c., and the brisk programme of building which accompanied the 1888 World Exhibition, led to an unprecedented boom in Modernisme building, much of which still dominates Barcelona today. Typical of the style is the way it turns to a free expression of architectural form, increasingly ignoring straight lines and symmetry and indulging – perhaps to excess – in decorative, playful and even comical detail. The manner in which it grew was largely due to the fact that – unlike so many previous art trends, which were largely seen only in buildings frequented by an élite and wealthy upper class – it was encountered by all classes in the course of their daily lives; in religious and secular buildings open to the public at large, in purpose-built and functional structures and even in such comparatively commonplace areas as offices and shops. The boundaries between architecture and the fine arts became fluid; many an edifice in the Modernisme style looks more like a giant sculpture than a building.

That which perhaps makes Modernisme appear somewhat strange to those of us from the main continent of Europe, the United Kingdom or indeed elsewhere in the world is the above-mentioned mix of different styles, together with an obvious tendency to over-ornateness and clutter. Quite often we find that Gothic, Moorish and Baroque features are the bed-fellows of winding and prolific Art Nouveau botanical shapes and designs, sometimes even on buildings of very cramped dimensions.

Almost everywhere we find buildings by Antoni Gaudí (1852–1926), the man who left the strongest imprint on Barcelona's skyline. In addition to his masterpiece, the Temple de la Sagrada Família, mention must also be made of the many buildings he designed for his generous patron Eusebi Güell (see Famous People), including Casa Milà, Casa Batlló and Casa Vicens. Many of Barcelona's squares and boulevards are illuminated by candelabras designed by him, and the ornamental pavements in many parts of Eixample are also his work.

Of equal importance is Lluis Domènech i Montaner (1850–1920: see Famous People), who was responsible for an impressive number of functional buildings, mainly for the 1888 World Exhibition, as well as the magnificent Palau de la Música Catalana. Somewhat less spectacular are the designs of Josep Puig i Cadalfach (1867–1957: see Famous People).

The blocks of houses on either side of the Passeig de Gracia contain the largest concentration of Modernistic buildings. This area has been named the Quadrat d'Or ("The Golden Rectangle") and placed under a preservation order.

Quadrat d'Or

The buildings mentioned above have been clearly indicated in the "Barcelona from A to Z" section of this guide.

SANT
GERVASI

Pl. de
Joan Carles I

Parc del
Poeta
E. Marquina

Piscines
i Esports

Pl. de
Francesc Macià

Diagonal

Sarrià

Diagonal

Hospital Clínic

Sagrat
Cor

Universitat
Industrial

Sem

Ud

EIXAMPLE

Pl. del
Papa
Rius XIII

Zona
Universitaria

LES CORTS

Estació
Central de Sants

Plaça de
Toros
Les Arenes

Sants

Creu Coberta

Plaça
d'Espanya

Palau de
Congressos

Palau
Municipal
d'Esports

Franca Xica

Mu
Arque

Poble
Espanyol

Palau Nacional

Estadi
Olímpic

Sant Feliu de Llobregat

Av. Carrilet

Av. Carrilet

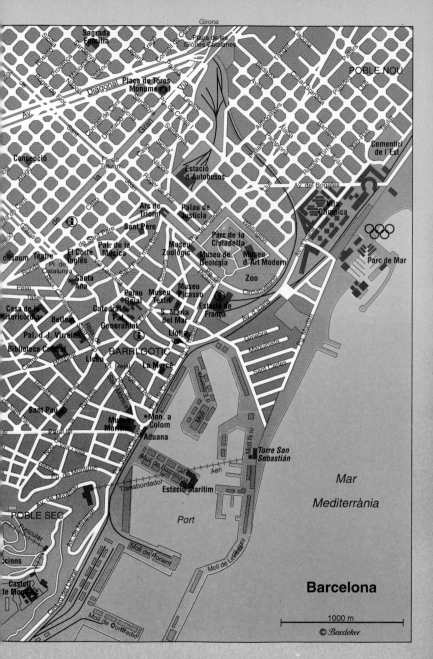

Barcelona

Barcelona from A to Z

Notes

At the time when research was being undertaken for this book, vast areas of
the city centre as well as many of the main sights were undergoing far-
reaching renovations and refurbishments to coincide with the Olympics
and the quincentenary of the discovery of America. As a result no absolute
guarantee can be given for the accuracy of the detailed descriptions that
follow, with regard to opening times, building works and general accessi-
bility, even though on-the-spot investigations were conducted with the
utmost care. Where the existence of such alterations has been established
with certainty, annotations to this effect are to be found by the relevant
names in red print.

City plans

Most commercial plans of the City of Barcelona and also the large plan
contained in this guidebook are normally not orientated towards the north,
but are printed in such a way that, for example, the streets in the extension
of the city area known as "Eixample" runs parallel to the grid of the plan.
This can be somewhat confusing and may cause a visitor difficulty in
getting his bearings.

The correct topographical situation can be seen on the small general plan
on pages 36 and 37.

The co-ordinates printed in capital letters against the main headings refer
to the large city plan at the end of this guide; co-ordinates in small letters
refer to the insert detailed plan. (Example: Cathedral J–K 4 · c 2.)

The names of streets and Metro (underground) stations in Barcelona are
signed exclusively in Catalan, as are almost all public buildings, monuments, etc. Consequently in the following chapter the names of such places
also only appear in Catalan.
The names of Metro and railway stations dispense with specific expressions such as "Plaça" (= square), "Carrer" (= street), "Passeig" (= promenade) or "Avinguda" (= avenue); therefore when referring to these the
same principle applies: for example the Avinguda del Paral.lel is referred to
by the shortened form "Paral.lel". This actually matches standard postal
practice.

City centre
transport

Thanks to the frequency of its services and the compactness of its network,
the Metro (underground) is the most comfortable of the public transport
methods available. In addition, however, buses and trains (Ferrocarrils de
la Generalitat de Catalunya) operate services in the city centre area, starting
points for which are in the Plaça de Catalunya (Plaça d'Espanya for trains to
Montserrat).

Antic Hospital

See Hospital de la Santa Creu

Arc de Triomf   L 4

The Arc de Triomf (triumphal arch) forms the main architectural feature of
the spacious Passeig de Lluís Companys, which runs from the Parc de la

Location Passeig de
Lluís Companys

◀ View of Montjuïc from the Columbus Monument

Arc de Triomf, main gateway to the World Exhibition of 1888

Metro
Arc de Triomf (L1)

Ciutadella(see entry) in a north-westerly direction. It was erected as the prestigious main gateway for the World Exhibition of 1888 by Josep Vilaseca. The brickwork incorporates elements of Moorish style; the reliefs depict allegories of trade, industry, agriculture and art. It has recently been restored at a cost of 120 million pesetas.

Archaeological Museum

See Museu Arqueològic

Architects' Society Building   J 4 · c 3

Location
Plaça Nova

Metro
Liceu (L3)

Opposite the main façade of the cathedral (see entry) and on the far side of the Plaça Nova stands the Col.legi d'Arquitectes (Society of Architects). The building, one of the first high-rise blocks in the city, was erected in 1962. On the side overlooking the square there is a triptych of graffiti friezes based on sketches by Pablo Picasso. The middle section depicts the "Gegants" (larger-than-life human figures who are led out at popular festivals) and figures with palm branches; the left-hand section (on the Carrer dels Arcs) symbolises the joy of life, while the right-hand section (on the Carrer dels Capellans) shows the "frieze of standards". Inside the building are two more wall paintings by Picasso.

Badalona   outside the area of the city plan

Location
to the north-east

The industrial town of Badalona (pop. approximately 200,000) lies to the north-east of Barcelona and on the far side of the Riu Besos. Today Badalona has become practically part of the Catalan capital.

Graffiti, based on a Picasso drawing, on the Society of Architects Building

The city area extends some 5km/3 miles along the flat coastline. The quality of the sea water suffers in this area as a result of emissions from the thriving industries. In the old town centre stands the Church of Santa Maria, dating from the 17th c. (works by the Baroque painter Antoni Viladomat). Roman remains are to be found in the town's Archaeological Museum (Museu de Badalona, Plaça Assemblea de Catalunya 1).

Metro
Joan XXIII,
Sant Roc,
Gorg, Pep Ventura
(L4)

About 3km/2 miles to the north-west of Badalona lies Sant Jeroni de la Murtra, which with its former monastery, built in the 14th c. (15th c. cloister), is a favoured destination for outings from the town.

Sant Jeroni de la Murtra

About 3km/2 miles to the north-east of the town, in Montgat, is a castle which played an important part in the War of Liberation fought against Napoleon (1788–1808).

Montgat

Barceloneta (city district)

K–L 2

The district of Barceloneta ("Little Barcelona") extends to the north-east of the harbour basin, which separates it from the sea. It was built from 1753 onwards and was laid out with a regular ground plan of intersecting streets crossing one another at right angles – a typical Baroque arrangement. Philip V's victory over the Catalans (1714) and the building of the Citadel (see Parc de la Ciutadella) had already taken place. Barceloneta was intended to provide new dwellings for those citizens who hitherto had lived on the site of the Citadel. Even today Barceloneta is above all others the area of the city with a pronounced maritime character; here is the Museu Marítim (see entry) and a number of good fish restaurants.

Location
north-east of the
port

Metro
Barceloneta (L4)

On the Plaça de la Barceloneta stands the Church of Sant Miquel del Port, which dates from the district's beginnings and which, in the arrangement

Sant Miquel

41

of its floor space and façades, has strong affinities with the Italian Baroque style. To the right of the church façade is the house where Ferdinand de Lesseps lived in 1858 (memorial plaque).

Beach

The wide Passeig Marítim runs along Barceloneta's seashore. Stretching out to the north-east, the beach, with its broad expanses of fine sand, is a very popular place for relaxation and recreation. Care is taken to maintain the quality of the water at a high level, despite the beach's proximity to the city and its industrial installations.

Parc de Mar

The Parc de Mar, a spacious area of land in the north-east corner of Barceloneta, is where the Olympic Village, with its pair of distinctive high-rise towers, has been built. The yachting harbour of Nova Icaria is also located there.

Passeig Nacional

The Passeig Nacional, which separates Barceloneta from the rest of the port area, leads from the Moll de Barceloneta southwards to the Torre de San Sebastián, a 96m/315ft high steel pylon which is the terminus for the harbour cable car (see Port) from Montjuïc (see entry).

Barri Gòtic (city district)   J–K 3–4 · b–c 1–3

Location
north-east of the Ramblas

The Barri Gòtic (the "Gothic quarter") extends from the port to the cathedral and from the Ramblas as far as the Via Laietana. It is the oldest part of the city and acquired its distinctive character chiefly during the Gothic period when Barcelona, Genoa and Venice were the most important merchant cities in the Mediterranean and possessed untold riches. However the roots of the city can be traced back to Roman times. Parts of the city wall date from this period and numerous remains of it can be seen.

For two thousand years the Barri Gòtic has been the spiritual and secular heart of the city. On Mont Tabor, at 12m/40ft the highest point in the old city, stands the cathedral, surrounded by narrow medieval alleys. Close by lived the Counts of Barcelona and the Kings of Catalonia and Aragón. Christopher Columbus was received here by the Catholic Monarchs after his first voyage of discovery, and since the 14th and 15th c. the city and provincial administrations have had their seat here. Today the Barri Gòtic is mainly pedestrianised, with many shops selling fashion goods, jewellery, antiques, books, souvenirs, ceramics, textiles, leather goods, etc.; there are also a number of small bars and restaurants.

Tour of the Barri Gòtic

The starting point of the suggested tour of the Barri Gòtic is the Plaça Sant Jaume, where stand the Casa de la Ciutat and the Palau de la Generalitat (see entries). The first building on the left in Carrer Jaume I houses the Museu d'Holografia (see entry). A short way east, on the far side of the Plaça de Sant Just, is the Galeria de Catalans Il.lustres (see entry).
From the Plaça Sant Jaume we continue north-west between the Palau de la Generalitat and the Casa dels Canonges (canons' house) to the cathedral cloister (see entry), and the Casa de l'Ardiaca, (archdeacon's house) where the Institut Municipal d'Història has its headquarters. Old Roman town walls can be seen by the Palau Episcopal (bishop's palace) behind which lies the picturesque little Plaça de Sant Felip Nerí, with the Museu de Calçat (footwear museum), while to the north, on the far side of the Plaça Nova, stands the modern building of the Architects Society, with its well-known Picasso graffiti.
The Plaça de la Seu (cathedral square) is bordered on the north by the Casa Pia Almoina. Following the north-east wall of the Cathedral we reach the Museu Frederic Marès and further on the Museu d'Història de la Ciutat (see entries) and the adjoining Plaça del Rei (King's Square); the latter is flanked by fine old buildings. We return to the Plaça de Sant Jaume or to the Metro station at the Plaça del Angel.

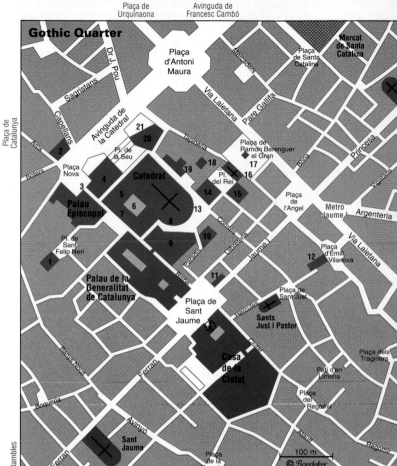

1 Museu del Calçat (Footwear Museum)
2 Architects' Building
3 Towers of Roman city wall
4 Archdeacon's House (Institut Municipal d'Història)
5 Roman Gateway
6 Cathedral Cloister
7 Porta de Santa Eulària
8 Porta de la Pietat (entrance to cloister)
9 Canons' House
10 Pillars of Temple of Augustus (inside)
11 Museu d'Holografie
12 Galería de Catalana Il-lustres
13 Porta de Sant Iu
14 Palau de Llochtinent (Archive of the Crown of Aragón)
15 Palau Clariana Padellás (Museu d'Història de la Ciutat)
16 Capella de Santa Agata
17 Equestrian statue of Ramon Berenguer the Great
18 Saló de Tinell
19 Museu Frederic Marès
20 Casa Pia Almoina
21 Roman city walls

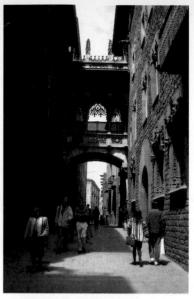

Streets in the Old Town . . .   *. . . and in the Gothic Quarter*

Barri Xino (city district)   H–J 3–4 · a–b 2–3

Location
between the
Ramblas and
Paral.lel

To the south-west of the Barri Gòtic extends a continuation of the old part of the city – the Barri Xino (Chinese quarter). With its maze of narrow streets and alleyways this part of the city is to a large extent in urgent need of redevelopment and is a centre for prostitution, drug trafficking and petty crime and, after dark at least, should be avoided.

Biblioteca de Catalunya. See entry

Hospital de la Santa Creu. See entry

Sant Pau del Camp. See entry

Biblioteca de Catalunya   H–J 4 · a 3

Location
Carrer del Carme

Metro
Liceu (L3)

The Biblioteca de Catalunya is housed in one part of the former Hospital de la Santa Creu. The library, which was founded in 1914, today contains around a million volumes as well as a special section on the works of Miguel Cervantes Saavedra, the author of "Don Quixote".

Proceeding from the Carrer del Carme, the visitor turns right and comes to a gateway. The large colourful picture tiles, depicting scenes from the life of St Paul, are worthy of note. There are also brightly coloured tiled decorations in the inner courtyard (with its two-storey arcades and a statue of St Paul from the 17th c.) and on the staircase. The reading room is only open to registered users.

Other libraries

This group of buildings also houses the Biblioteca Infantil Santa Creu (children's library) and the Biblioteca Popular Sant Pau (public library) as well as part of the University Library.

Botanical Garden   E 4

Behind the Palau Nacional (see entry) and forming part of the park of
Montjuïc (see entry) extends the Botanical Garden (Catalan: Jardí Botànic)
with its beautiful flora. It was laid out immediately after the World Exhibition of 1929 on a site which included an abandoned quarry, and by virtue of
this location it possesses a range of microclimatic zones which can even
offer good conditions of growth to exotic plants. Otherwise the stocks of
plants are mainly arranged according to a geographical standpoint. The
garden is one of the most important examples of its type in Spain.

Close by is the sports area, which has been greatly extended for the
Olympics (see Olympic Sites). A concrete bridge has been built across the
Botanical Garden on which stands the bronze statue of a man bearing
the Olympic torch.

The gardens are linked to the Institut i Jardí Botànic (Botanical Institute and
Gardens) a new botanic garden laid out between the Olympic Stadium and
Castell de Montjuïc (see Montjuïc). Information about the garden can be
obtained from the reception centre situated at the entrance, near the Olym-
pic Stadium.
Open: Summer: Mon.–Sat. 3–7pm, Sun. and public holidays 9am–2pm.
Winter: Mon.–Sat. 3–5pm, Sun and public holidays 9am–2pm.

Location
Montjuïc

Metro
Plaça d'Espanya
(L1, L3)

Bus
61 (from Plaça
Espanya)

Institut i Jardí
Botànic

---

*Casa Batlló   J 6

The Casa Batlló, situated at the crossroads of the Passeig de Gràcia and the
Carrer Aragó, was designed by Antoni Gaudí for the textile manufacturer
Josep Batlló i Casanovas and counts as one of the most famous buildings
of the Modernist school.

The appearance of the façade is characterised by an ornamental structure
which seems to have departed completely from any received principles of
architecture. The window frontage on the first floor is bordered by freely
swinging shapes some of which suggest plants, others entrances to caves.
Above that the façade is covered with glazed ceramic tiles in green, blue
and ochre colours. The small balconies have railings made out of beaten
steel. The wave-shaped roof has, like that of the Casa Milà (see entry), a
large number of richly decorated chimneys. Parts of the interior fittings,
which were likewise designed by Gaudí, can be seen in the Museu Gaudí
(see entry).

In order to view the interior of the Casa Batlló (at present partially undergoing reconstruction), it is necessary to obtain permission from the Càtedra Gaudí (see Practical Information).

On the left of the Casa Batlló protrudes the Casa Ametller (1900), a house
built by Josep Puig i Cadafalch in Neo-Gothic forms, and at the south-
eastern end of the street intersection (the crossing with the Carrer Consell
de Cent) stands the Casa Lleó Morera (1905; recently restored and now the
premises of the Patronat de Turisme de Barcelona), the work of Lluís
Domènech i Montaner. Because of the unconventional and totally distinctive character of each of the three buildings, the group is referred to as
the "mansana de la discòrdia" ("apple of discord"), where the play on
words depends on the double meaning of the word "mansana" ("block of
houses" as well as "apple").

Location
Passeig de
Gràcia 43

Metro
Gràcia (L3, L4)

Mansana de la
Discòrdia

Casa Calvet   K 5 · d 4

The Casa Calvet (1898–1900), not far north of the Plaça de Catalunya, was
also designed by Antoni Gaudí. Compared to his other work it is spartan in
the meagre decoration of the façade. For this building Gaudí was awarded
the architectural prize of the City of Barcelona.
The furnishings, some of which are also by Gaudí, can be seen in the Gaudí
Museum (see Parc Güell); the interior of the Casa Calvet is not open to the
public, as the building is privately owned.

Location
Carrer Casp 48

Metro
Urquinaona (L1, L4)

Casa de Caritat   J 4 · b 3

The Casa de Caritat is situated in the old area of the city to the south of the
Plaça de Catalunya. Since the 13th c. the area has belonged to the Augusti-
nian canons and later a seminary was set up there. The cloister acquired its
present appearance, which follows Tuscan models, in the middle of the
18th c. Today the Casa de Caritat has been enlarged by a modern extension
and serves as a cultural centre and exhibition hall.

Location
Carrer Montalegre

Metro
Catalunya (L1, L3),
Universitat (L1)

It is intended to use the Casa de la Caritat to house the collection of
contemporary art which lack of space prevents being shown in the Museu
d'Art Modern (see entry).

Museu d'Art
Contemporani

The Carrer Montalegre ends to the south of Plaça dels Angels. Here
stands the former convent of the same name which was erected in 1560 in
the very late Gothic style. At the present time it is undergoing conversion
for use as a central library for the City Museum.

Els Angels

Casa de la Ciutat   J 3 · c 2

On the south-east side of the Plaça de Sant Jaume, which forms the centre
of the Barri Gòtic (see entry), stands the Casa de la Ciutat (city hall). This
magnificent building, which dates originally from the 14th c., possesses
side façades which are still in part Gothic, whilst the main façade was
rebuilt in 1847 by Josep Mas in the Classical style. The inner courtyard with
its beautiful flight of steps is worth seeing.
Inside the City Hall is the great Saló de Cent (council chamber; 14th c.) with
wall hangings in the Catalan colours of red and yellow. There is also the
Saló de les Cròniques with its marble flooring by Josep Maria Sert.

Location
Plaça de Sant
Jaume

Metro
Liceu (L3),
Jaume I (L4)

On the ground floor of the City Hall is the Oficina Municipal d'Informació
(City Tourist Information Office) where information of all kinds is
obtainable.

Tourist
Information

Casa de l'Ardiaca

See Institut Municipal d'Història.

Casa Lleó Morera

See Casa Batlló

◀ *A building as art – the Casa Batilló*

Casa de la Ciutat, the City Hall

**Casa Milà   K 6

Location
Passeig de
Gràcia 92

Metro
Diagonal (L3, L5)

The Casa Milà, situated on a corner site at the crossing of the Passeig de Gràcia with the Carrer de Provença, is the last and most famous secular building of Antoni Gaudí. In the design of this multi-storeyed dwelling block he departed completely from established principles of construction, so that the result resembles a piece of sculpture rather than a functional building. The observer will search in vain for absolute straight lines; instead the façade of carved natural stone displays rounded windows, metal balcony railings twining around in plant-like shapes and a curved roof-line on which the many chimneys confer a formal rather than a functional character.

The complete building is grouped around two oval-shaped air wells. Even when it was being erected the building aroused passionate controversy: serious differences arose between Gaudí and his client Milà i Camps-Segimon on account of the long construction period and the alterations which Gaudí continually kept putting off making. It was also not long before the building acquired the derisive nick-name of "Pedrera" (quarry). Recently the façade was thoroughly cleaned and the rest of the building is at present being restored. On the ground floor there are offices of the Caixa de Catalunya, which is responsible for the conservation of the building, and some shops. The interior of the building is not open to the general public.

Guided tours
Mon.–Fri. 10 and
11am, noon and 1,
4, 6 and 6pm;
Sat. 10 and 11am,
noon and
1pm; Sun. 11am,
noon and 1pm

By following a guided tour the visitor can see the patios, terrace and roof of the Casa Milà. The entrance is on the Carrer de Provença, from which the inner courtyard is reached through a remarkable wrought-iron gate. A narrow stairway leads up to the roof truss. Its load-bearing construction of narrow tiled ribs running in vertical parallel arches bears witness to Gaudí's genius as a structural engineer.

Details . . .   *. . . of the Casa Milà*

Casa Milà in the Passeig de Gràcia

The roof area itself is then reached, with its numerous strangely shaped chimneys partly covered in mosaics. A walk around up here also rewards the visitor with beautiful views across the city (the Sagrada Família in the distance to the north-east).

Casa-Museu Verdaguer   outside the area of the city plan

Location
Vil.la Joana
(Vallvidrera)

Railway
(FF.CC. de la
Generalitat)
Baixador de
Vallvidrera

Open
Tues.–Sun.
9am–2pm
(closed Mon.)

The Vil.la Joana, which has been converted into a museum for the Catalan poet Jacint Verdaguer, is situated in the north-west outskirts of the city in the district of Vallvidrera at the southern foot of Mt Tibidabo. It is best reached by taking the train from the Plaça de Catalunya (see entry) in the direction of Sant Cugat (Ferrocarrils de la Generalitat) as far as the Station Baixador de Vallvidrera; from here the museum is reached after a five-minute walk in a south-easterly direction.

The villa was originally a manor house, partly dating back to the Middle Ages. Its owners gave the ailing Verdaguer shelter here. After a few weeks the poet died on the 10 June 1902 at the age of 57.

The museum partly occupies rooms used by Verdaguer and subsequently kept virtually unaltered, and displays original manuscripts as well as contemporary paintings and drawings. A large part is devoted to Verdaguer's epic poem "L'Atlàntida", for which the painter F. Vall Verdaguer has painted a series of oil pictures. A visual and aural commentary completes the overview of Verdaguer's life and work.

In a pine wood nearby is the "Font Vella" (old spring).

*Casa Vicens   K 8

Location
Carrer Carolines
18–24

Metro
Lesseps (L3)

The Casa Vicens, situated in a narrow side-street off the Carrer Gran de Gràcia, was built by Gaudí between 1883 and 1888 for the ceramics manufacturer Manuel Vicens i Montaner and is one of the earliest of the architect's designs to be realised. The still largely linear conception shows the strong influence of the Moorish-Spanish architectural tradition, and this impression is strengthened by the generous use of tiled decoration. The property is separated from the street by a metal fence consisting of stylised fan palm leaves.

The interior of the Casa Vicens is not open to the public.

Catalunya en Miniatura   outside the area of the city plan

Location
in Torrelles de
Llobregat
(17km/10½ miles
south)

The model layout Catalunya en Miniatura (Catalonia in miniature) is situated 17km/10½ miles south of the city centre. The best approach by car is on the Martorell road as far as Molins del Relund, continuing via Vincenç dels Horts. The feature includes models (on a scale of 1:25) of the most important monuments and buildings in Catalonia.
Bus: "Tisa" line from corner of Viriat and Numància.
Open: Daily 9am–7pm.

**Cathedral   J–K 4 · c 2

Location
Plaça de la Seu

On Monte Tabor, which at 12m/40ft is the highest point in the Barri Gòtic (see entry), stands the cathedral (Santa Creu or Santa Eulàlia). It was begun

Casa Vicens . . .   *. . . and details of the façade*

in 1298 on the site of an old Romanesque building, of which a few stone reliefs are still preserved at the north-east doorway. By 1448 it was completed except for the main façade and the dome, which were added in 1898 and 1913.

The layout of the cathedral is rather unusual: the apse and altar area lie to the south-east whilst the main façade faces north-west.

Coming from the Plaça Sant Jaume, the visitor arrives at the very beautiful cloister (Claustre) with its magnolias and palms. It is entered by the Portal de Santa Eulàlia. The cloister dates from 1380–1451 and is lined with numerous chapels containing the altars of various saints. Of note is the fountain which is crowned by a small statue of St George (Sant Jordi) with the dragon. At Corpus Christi there is a custom of blowing an egg and letting it spin on the fountain. There is a special explanation for the geese which inhabit the cloister: in the Middle Ages they guarded the cathedral and its treasures, for their aggressiveness and vociferousness have been well known since the averted storming of the Roman Capitol (A.D. 387), and this tradition lives on today.
In the south-western corner of the cloister is the Capella de Santa Llucia, founded in 1270, and next to it the museum.

The cathedral museum (Museu de la Catedral) in the former chapter room (Sala Capitular) displays paintings by Spanish masters from the 15th and 16th c., sculptures and liturgical articles.

The High Gothic interior (83.3m/273ft long, 37.2m/122ft wide, 25.5m/84ft high) is divided into three aisles. The main aisle and side aisles of the cathedral are approximately the same height. High up there is a row of small windows. On the side aisles underneath the low galleries are chapels, mainly from the 16th and 17th c. and with ornate Baroque altars. The most

Metro
Jaume I (L4)

Open
Cathedral: daily
7.30am–1.30pm
and 4–7.30pm;
Cloister: daily.
8.45am–1.30pm
and 4–7pm;
Museum: daily
11am–1pm
Cloister

Museum

Cathedral interior

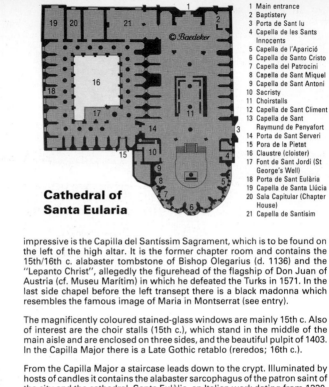

1 Main entrance
2 Baptistery
3 Porta de Sant Iu
4 Capella de les Sants Innocents
5 Capella de l'Aparició
6 Capella de Santo Cristo
7 Capella del Patrocini
8 Capella de Sant Miquel
9 Capella de Sant Antoni
10 Sacristy
11 Choirstalls
12 Capella de Sant Climent
13 Capella de Sant Raymund de Penyafort
14 Porta de Sant Serveri
15 Pora de la Pietat
16 Claustre (cloister)
17 Font de Sant Jordi (St George's Well)
18 Porta de Sant Eulària
19 Capella de Santa Llúcia
20 Sala Capitular (Chapter House)
21 Capella de Santisim

Cathedral of Santa Eularia

impressive is the Capilla del Santíssim Sagrament, which is to be found on the left of the high altar. It is the former chapter room and contains the 15th/16th c. alabaster tombstone of Bishop Olegarius (d. 1136) and the "Lepanto Christ", allegedly the figurehead of the flagship of Don Juan of Austria (cf. Museu Marítim) in which he defeated the Turks in 1571. In the last side chapel before the left transept there is a black madonna which resembles the famous image of Maria in Montserrat (see entry).

The magnificently coloured stained-glass windows are mainly 15th c. Also of interest are the choir stalls (15th c.), which stand in the middle of the main aisle and are enclosed on three sides, and the beautiful pulpit of 1403. In the Capilla Major there is a Late Gothic retablo (reredos; 16th c.).

Crypt

From the Capilla Major a staircase leads down to the crypt. Illuminated by hosts of candles it contains the alabaster sarcophagus of the patron saint of the city and the cathedral, Santa Eulàlia, an Italian work dating from 1330.

Cathedral treasury

In the sacristy the cathedral treasury (Catalan, tresor), which includes gold and silver articles and an alabaster image of the Madonna and rosary, is worth seeing

Tower

From the south-west tower of the cathedral (210 steps; access from inside the building) there is a very rewarding view of the city, its hinterland and the sea.

Casa de l'Ardiaca

See Institut Municipal d'Història

Palau Episcopal

See entry

Centre Permanent d'Artesania   J 6

Location
Passeig de
Gràcia 55

Metro
Gràcia (L3, L4)

In recent years Barcelona has developed into a notable design centre. The Centre Permanent d'Artesania has in three rooms exhibitions and displays on various topics and themes (open during shopping hours). As a result of European regions having gained more importance, close co-operation has also existed with the Rhône-Alpes area of France and Baden-Württemberg in Germany, especially with the Stuttgart provincial inspectorate

Col.legi d'Arquitectes

See Architects' Society Building

Col.legi de les Teresianes   G 9

The Col.legi de les Teresianes is the parent convent of the sisterhood of Teresa, which takes its name from St Teresa of Avila (1515–82).

The building of the college had already been started when in 1888 Antoni Gaudí was commissioned to complete it.

Measured against other works by the architect the Col.legi de les Teresianes is of unwonted sobriety – a concession to the rule of the order. The brick-built pointed arches of the façade, particularly on the top storey, point to Gothic models.

The buildings house a school and therefore access to the public is limited.

Location
Carrer Ganduxer
95–105

Railway station
(FF.CC.)
Bonanova

Open
Sat. 11am–1pm
(except in summer)

*Colonia Güell   outside the area of the city plan

In 1898 Count Eusebi Güell, the great patron of Antoni Gaudí, had a social settlement laid out for the workers in his textile factory in Santa Coloma del Cervelló. the Colnia Güell. Gaudí was commissioned to build a church for the settlement and his preliminary sketches reveal a startling similarity with the Sagrada Família (see entry). However the church in the workers' settlement was actually not built in the same style as the latter.

The lower part of the planned church, the so-called crypt, was constructed between 1908 and 1916 on a pine-clad hill. In its design two aspects are clearly visible: on the one hand the static and formal structural details of Gothic – in so far as these were adopted by Gaudí – and on the other hand the principle of "oblique supports" which he introduced, and which, together with parabolic enclosing arches, permits a spatial design free from all restraints. The mosaics, especially the one above the main doorway, are particularly noteworthy. The pews in the church were also designed by Gaudí.

Location
Santa Coloma del
Cervelló

Railway station
(Ferrocarrils de la
Generalitat)
From Plaça
d'Espanya to Molí
Nou

Open
Mon.–Fri.
10.15am–1.15pm
and 4–6pm (closed
Thur. pm);
Sun. and public
holidays
10am–1.30pm

Costa Daurada   outside the area of the city plan

The term "Costa Daurada" (Span. Costa Dorada = golden coast) refers to the stretch of coastline between the mouth of the River Tordera (which also

General

The Cathedral . . .   *. . . and the Gran Teatre del Liceu (p. 64)*

here forms the border between the provinces of Barcelona and Girona) and the delta of the River Ebre (Span. Ebro) to the south of Tarragona. This area, which extends along about 260km/162 miles of the Mediterranean coast, is well-known for its gently sloping beaches and its fine, golden-coloured sand, as well as being valued for its mild climate.

Within the province of Barcelona, Sitges and Vilanova i La Geltrú deserve special mention.

Sitges

Railway station (RENFE) from Central-Sants or Passeig de Gràia to Sitges (45 mins)

About 37km/23 miles to the south-west of Barcelona, Sitges is one of the oldest Spanish coastal resorts. Even nowadays it is less subject to mass tourism than other places and moreover is patronised by a discerning and well-to-do clientele with cultural demands. Many residents of Barcelona have second homes here. The British writer G. K. Chesterton invented his character Father Brown here.

Worth visiting is the Museu Cau Ferrat (housed in the former home of the art collector Santiago Rusiñol) with its collection of Modernist art, paintings by Picasso and El Greco and others. Attached to the same building is the Museu Maricel de Mar (furniture, glass and ceramics going back as far as the Middle Ages; paintings by Josep Maria Sert).

In a patrician house dating from the late 18th c. is housed the Museu Romàntic (furniture and a collection of dolls).

Within the municipality of Sitges are the three sporting harbours of Aiguadolç, Garraf and Port Ginestra.

Gran Casino

The Gran Casino de Barcelona is located in Sitges.

Vilanova i La Geltrú

A short distance to the south-west of Sitges lies the busy commercial centre of Vilanova i La Geltrú. In the Castell (13th c. castle) there is a museum of art. The Casa Papiol on the Carrer Major, with all its upper-class furnishings, is now a museum open to the public.

Situated close to the railway station is the museum named after its founder, the Catalan minister and poet Victor Balaguer (d. 1901) (antiquities; paintings, including an Annunciation by El Greco; a small ethnographic collection).
Near the harbour, on the Carrer Almiral Cervera, is the novel Museu Curiositats Marineres with all kinds of oddities connected with the sea.

Drassanes

See Museu Marítim.

Eglesia de Betlem   J 4 · b 3

At the crossing of the Rambla dels Estudis with the Carrer del Carme is to be seen the Baroque façade of the Eglesia de Betlem, built between 1681 and 1732, formerly a Jesuit church. It is characterised by its heavily embossed stonework. In the entrance portal are portrayed Ignatius of Loyola, the founder of the order, Francesco Borgia, the third general of the Jesuit order, as well as the birth of Christ. The rich Baroque furnishings and decorations inside the church were completely destroyed by fire in 1938; their restoration in unadorned Classical forms is artistically of little significance.

Location
Rambla dels
Estudis

Metro
Liceu (L3)

Opposite the side façade of the church and on the other side of the Rambla stands the Palau Moja, a palace which has reverted to its Baroque origins.

Palau Moja

Eglesia de la Concepció   J 6

One would never expect to find a Gothic church here in this extension of the city which was laid out after 1860 and in fact the Eglesia de la Concepció (Church of the Conception) was built in 1293 in the Barri Gòtic (see entry). Between 1871 and 1888 it was dismantled stone by stone and transported to its present-day location. The single-aisled interior is flanked by chapels; the attractive cloister dates from the 14th c.

Location
Rambla de
Catalunya

Metro
Diagonal (L3, L5)

Eixample (city district)

The district of Eixample (the name means "extension") extends in an arc round the old part of the city (see Barri Gòtic and Barri Xino) out as far as the foothills of Tibidabo (see entry) and Carmel. It is distinguished by a right-angled street network which passes through the characteristic "mansanas" (dwelling blocks) with their diagonal intersections.

Location
to the north and
west of the old city

Until the mid-19th c. the city boundaries were the limits of what was the still partially walled old quarter, with undeveloped land extending out to what were then the neighbouring localities. With the repeal of the Catalans' special privileges by Philip V (1714) and the loss of its Mediterranean pre-eminence Barcelona had entered a phase of economic decline which excluded any possibility of growth.
This changed with the reawakening of the Catalan national consciousness, which in 1814 led to the "Renaixença" (renaissance) when, in the wake of the Romantic movement and influenced by the Wars of Liberation of the time, there was a reawareness emerging in regions all over Europe of their history and culture. At the same time the growth of industry initiated a new era of upper-class prosperity, which did not leave the city's planning unaffected. In 1860 the old city walls of Barcelona were torn down and the

History

built-up areas expanded at an incredible rate partly as a result of the incorporation of several neighbouring places.

Pla Cerdà

When the extension of the city was beginning there was controversy among various town-planners concerning the best possible contemporary, and at the same time most sensible, design. Finally two alternatives remained: a plan by the architect Antoni Rovira i Trias, based on a network of streets radiating from the Old Town, and a checkerboard plan by Ildefons Cerdà.

At first the technical commission responsible decided on Rovira's project, but by a royal decree of 31 May 1860 the "Pla Cerdà" was adopted.

The great achievement of the city planners lay in the fact that right from the start they were able to resist untrammelled new development and to follow a plan in the true sense of the word. Their aim was to create a large-scale urban structure permeated by light and air. The man who masterminded and initiated the new developments was the engineer Ildefons Cerdà, who was responsible for their underlying concept. The chessboard-patterned street network with its, even by today's standards, generously proportioned roads and its large (100m/382ft × 100m/382ft) blocks of buildings, made it possible to reach any destination within the new city without any loss of time. Thus it was that two magnificent boulevards were needed to intersect the area diagonally: the Avinguda de la Diagonal and the Avinguda de la Meridiana (running at 2°10′ longitude parallel to the Greenwich Meridian), their point of intersection forming the Plaça de les Glòries Catalanes. Whilst the Diagonal has been almost completely built through from the Zona Universitària in the west almost as far as the coast in the east, the Meridiana is without its final stretch between Glòries Catalanes and Ciutadella.

The original lithograph of the design for the city extension is on display in the Museu d'Història de la Ciutat (see entry).

Overall view

The extension of the city into the Eixample district coincided with the development of modernisme (see Facts and Figures, Modernisme). This style of art and architecture, associated above all with Barcelona, embraces every variation from late Historicism through to Art Nouveau and does so without undergoing the complete cultural break that, for instance occurred in Germany between the period of rapid industrial expansion and the later period. The new city area particularly attracted circles of well-off upper-class people, and architects like Antoni Gaudí, Lluís Domènech i Montaner and Josep Puig i Cadafalch, with their magnificent buildings, conferred on the Eixample its unmistakable charm. Also relevant is the fact that Spain was neutral in both world wars, while the Civil War (1936–39) was far from being able to inflict the same kind of damage as the bombing campaigns to which other Europeans countries were subjected from 1939 to 1945.

Most of the representative buildings of the Modernist period are to be found in the Quadrat d'Or (see entry), the area on either side of the Passeig de Gràcia between the Plaça de Catalunya and the Avinguda de la Diagonal. The most important places will be found in the index at the end of this book.

Exhibition Grounds   E–F 4–5

Location
Avinguda Reina
Maria Cristina

The exhibition grounds (Fira de Barcelona) extend across all the land between the Plaça d'Espanya (see entry) and the steps leading up to the Palau Nacional (see entry). The area is bisected by the Avinguda de la Reina Maria Cristina which is bordered by fountains illuminated after dark.

Metro
Plaça d'Espanya
(L1, L3)

Barcelona is the most important trade fair centre of the country, even outranking Madrid, and comparable with those in other countries. At present there are about 40 large international events held annually.

For further information about the Barcelona Fair and other regular events see Practical Information, Trade Fairs.

Finca Güell   E 9

The Finca Güell, built in 1884–87 by Antoni Gaudí for the Count Güell as a country residence outside what was then the built-up area of the city, today lies in the district of Pedralbes, one of Barcelona's most select residential areas, in the immediate vicinity of the Palau de Pedralbes. The property consists of three buildings: the single storey lodge to the left of the entrance, the large former stables and, attached to them, the round riding hall.

From a stylistic point of view the group of buildings is closely linked to the Casa Vicens (1883–88) (see entry) and, in common with that building, is reminiscent of the architecture of the Spanish Moorish period. The roofs of both the lodge and the riding hall are spanned by domes crowned with lanterns; the façades are covered in decorative tiles to which the window sections, executed in clinker brick, make an attractive contrast. Worthy of note are the elaborate openwork bricked ledges which surround the roof of the stables.

Especially impressive is the wrought-iron, 5m/16ft wide entrance gate which gets its name "dragon gate" from its main motif. It demonstrates particularly clearly the influences of Art Nouveau on the work of Gaudí. The interior of the Finca today houses the Càtedra Gaudí, an institution dedicated to the maintenance and preservation of the work of Antoni Gaudí

Location
Avinguda
Pedralbes 7

Metro
Palau Reial, Maria
Cristina (L3)

*Dragon gate

Exhibition Grounds
(Fira de Barcelona)

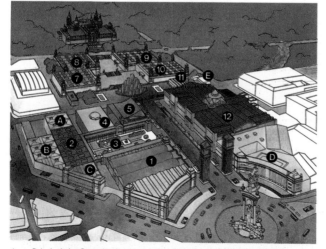

1	Palacio de las Comunicaciones	9/10	Palacio de Victoria Eugenia
2	Palacio del Cincuentenasio	11	Pabellón INI
3	Palacio del Universo	12	Palacio de la Metallurgía
4	Palacio Ferial		
5	Palacio de Congresos	A–D	Extensions
7/8	Palacio de Alfonso XIII	E	Pabellón van der Rohe

The Finca Güell, in the heart of the former estate

and from where permission to view some of these buildings can be obtained. (See Practical Information, Information.) Apart from this the estate is not open to the public.

Fira de Barcelona

See Exhibition Grounds

Fundació Antoni Tàpies   J 6

Location
Carrer Aragó 255

Metro
Passeig de Gràcia
(L3, L4)

Open
Tues.–Sun.
11am–8pm;
Closed Mon.

On the Carrer Aragó, not far to the south-west of where it crosses the Passeig de Gràcia, is the brick building designed in 1880–85 by Lluís Domènech i Montaner which used to be the premises of the publishing house of Montaner i Simon. Since 1984 it has been occupied by the Fundació Antoni Tàpies, a foundation established by this Barcelona artist who was born in the city in 1923. On the roof there is a surrealistic sculpture made of metal wires and bands.

The interior of the building has been emptied as far as possible in order to make space for the exhibitions. On the main level slightly below the entrance are temporary exhibitions while one level lower is the permanent exhibition which comprises a selection of Antoni Tàpies' graphic works. The gallery, supported by decorative cast-iron pillars and leaving the middle of the building clear rather in the manner of a Roman impluvium, is occupied by the well-stocked specialist library devoted to 20th c. art and Asian culture. The foundation possesses the most comprehensive collection of the artist's works and has taken on the role of a research centre for contemporary art.

The Dragon Gate of the Finca Güell ▶

Fundació Joan Miró

The Fundació Antoni Tàpies

Fundació Joan Miró   F 3

Location
Avinguda de
Miramar (Montjuïc)

Bus
61, then the
Funicular de
Montjuïc

Open
Tues., Wed., Fri.,
Sat.
11am–7pm; Thur.
11am–9.30pm;
Sun.and
public holidays
10.30 a.m.–2.30pm;
Closed Mon.

The Fundació Joan Miró nestles in park-like scenery on the north side of Montjuïc (see entry). It was here that the architects Josep Lluís Sert and Jaume Freixa erected a purpose-built home for the foundation established in 1971 by Joan Miró. The building, which was officially opened in 1988, is constructed in white concrete and comprises rigidly cubic elements, which on the inside are lit up by semi-circular skylights. There are two inner courtyards.

On the left of the entrance level, behind the ticket office, are the rooms reserved for short-term exhibitions of contemporary art, whilst the permanent exhibition occupies the right-hand part of the ground floor and the whole of the upper storey. The museum's exhibits comprise about 5000 items.

A tour of the Miró collection begins to the right of the first inner courtyard. Here there is first of all a chronological overview of the artist's life and work (examples of his work in reproduction form; model of the Spanish pavilion for the Paris World Exhibition of 1937) and also an enormous, brilliantly coloured wall tapestry. In the next passageway there is an original mercury fountain ("Font de Mercuri") by Alexander Calder. Then follows the plastic design for a group of figures in the Paris district of La Défense (in a coloured man-made substance) and after that a room with numerous monochrome graphics.
A staircase leads to the upper floor; here can be seen an extensive collection of paintings and there is a good view from above over the previously

Full "Flowing Metal" – the mercury fountain in the Fundació Joan Miró ▶

Fundació Joan Miró – inner courtyard . . .   *. . . and wall tapestry*

mentioned group of figures and the wall tapestry. In front of the entrance to the roof terrace (with its excellent view over the city and its coloured statues) stands the great marble "sun-bird"; this is followed by a series of original copper printing plates belonging to the "Mallorca" series. In the octagon are many small-scale graphics (starting in 1901 and displayed in choronological order clockwise). The collection is completed by some works by Miró's contemporaries (several Catalans; Alexander Calder, Max Ernst, Henry Moore, etc.)

In the upper part of the building is a library; a cafeteria and also a kiosk selling books and prints are located on the ground floor.

Gabinet de Física Experimental   H 13

Location
Carretera
Vallvidreraal-
Tibidabo

Open
By arrangement
(guided tours only)

The Gabinet de Física Experimental "Mentora Alsina" is on the road from Vallvidrera to Tibidabo (see entry), close to the lower station of the beach funicular which goes up the mountain.

The museum has its origins in the former private collection of Ferran Alsina i Perellada, who occupied the house until 1907, and it now belongs to the city of Barcelona. It has on display working models and originals of machines and instruments from the fields of mechanics, optics, acoustics, thermodynamics, electricity, etc.

Gabinet Numismàtic   J 4 · b 3

Location
Rambla 99

The Gabinet Numismàtic de Catalunya (gallery of coins) is housed in the Palau de la Virreina (see entry) on the Ramblas. As it is at the present time in the process of rearrangement, the collection is at the moment not generally open to the public.

Metro
Liceu (L3)

Temporarily closed

The museum's exhibits are derived from various private collections which since 1902 have come into the hands of the city either as gifts, bequests or loans. The collection numbers more than 10,000 items: medals, coins, banknotes and stocks and shares, mainly from Catalonia and going back to the 5th c. B.C. Of particular significance are the mintings from the Greek colony Emporion (Empúries) and Iberic, West Gothic and Roman coins, as well as coins from Latin America.

Gabinet Postal

See Palau de Pedralbes

Galeria de Catalans Il.lustres   K 3 · c 2

The Galeria de Catalans Il.lustres (Gallery of famous Catalans; part of the Museu d'Història de la Ciutat) is situated in the Barri Gòtic (see entry), only a few steps south of the Plaça de l'Angel and the metro station Jaume I. The building, the Gothic Palau Requesens, stands right on the Roman city wall and is at the same time the seat of the Acadèmia de Bones Lletres de Barcelona (Academy of Humanities).

Location
Carrer del Bisbe
Caçador 3

Metro
Jaume I (L4)

Open
By arrangement,
guided tours only
Tel. 3 15 11 11

The collection has some fifty portraits of Catalans who have made a contribution to literature, art, science and religion as well as in military affairs. Each portrait has a biographical overview with it.

Gran Casino de Barcelona

See Costa Daurada, Sitges

Gran Teatre del Liceu

See Liceu.

Hospital de la Santa Creu (Antic Hospital)   H–J 4 · a–b 2–3

In the middle of the Barri Xino (see entry), behind the market hall (see Mercat de Sant Josep), is the large complex of buildings, grouped around a cloistered courtyard, of the old Hospital de la Santa Creu (Holy Cross Hospital). It was founded in 1401 and not completed until the 17th c., which explains the varying architectural styles of the individual buildings.

Location
Carrer del Hospital

Metro
Liceu (L3)

From the Carrer del Hospital the building is entered by a 16th c. pair of doors, on the right-hand side of which stands the chapel. In the middle of the cloister there is a Baroque cross with a curved shaft, behind which is a large arch with a beautiful staircase. In the opposite building is housed a branch of the university library, while in the wings adjoining the Carrer del Carme the Biblioteca de Catalunya (see entry) is located.

About the turn of the century it became evident that the rooms of the Antic Hospital no longer answered its needs. The architect Lluís Domènech i Montaner was therefore commissioned to build a new up-to-date building in the Eixample district (see entry), the Hospital de la Santa Creu i de Sant Pau (see below).

Hospital de la Santa Creu i de Sant Pau   N 7–8

Location
Carrer Sant Antoni
Maria Claret

Metro
Hospital de Sant
Pau

At the beginning of the 20th c. the Hospital de la Santa Creu i de Sant Pau took over what had been up to then the role of the ancient Hospital de la Santa Creu (see above). To the north of the Sagrada Família (see entry), with which the site of the hospital is connected by the broad Avinguda de Gaudí, the architect Lluís Domènech i Montaner built a hospital complex which, in contradiction to established principles of construction, was not a unified single large building but combined on one single large site the various hospital departments, each housed in a pavilion and separated from the others by large expanses of grass. The buildings display characteristic modernistic façade decorations.

Institut Municipal d'Història   J 4 · c 2

Location
Carrer Santa
Llúcia 1

Metro
Jaume I (L4)

The Institut Municipal d'Història (City History Institute), founded in 1922, is housed in the beautiful Casa de l'Ardiaca (Archdeacon's House), part of which go back to the 12th c. and which essentially acquired the external appearance which it has today in the 15th c., during the Late Gothic period, whilst the decorative figures show the influence of the Italian Renaissance.

The interior of the building is only open to scientists; of note however is the inner courtyard, surrounded by arcades, with multi-coloured decorative tiles and a Gothic fountain.

Jardí Botànic

See Botanical Garden.

Jardins Mossèn Costa i Llobera

See Montjuïc.

Jardins Mossèn Jacint Verdaguer

See Montjuïc.

**Liceu   J 4 · b 2

Location
Rambla dels
Caputxins 65

Metro
Liceu (L3)

See picture (p. 54)

The Gran Teatre del Liceu (officially Liceo Filarmónico Dramático Barcelonés de Su Majestad la Reina Isabel) is the largest opera house in Spain and next to La Scala Milan the second largest traditional theatre in Europe. Built in 1844 and inaugurated in 1848 it conceals behind its somewhat plain façade a magnificent auditorium and 19th c. wall and ceiling paintings in New Pompeian style. Many boxes are privately owned which limits the number of tickets available to the public.
Open: Guided tours: Mon.–Fri. 11.30am and 12.15pm.

LLotja

See Stock Exchange

Mansana de la Discòrdie

See Casa Batlló

Marinemuseum

See Museu Marítim

Mercat del Born   K 3 · d 2

A short distance to the south-west of the Parc de la Ciutadella (see entry) and on the far side of the Passeig de Picasso stands the Mercat del Born, once the largest market hall in the city. It was built on a steel skeleton in 1873–76 from designs by the architects Antoni Rovira, Josep Fontserè and Josep Comet. Today the hall is used as a cultural centre with regular functions and temporary exhibitions.

Location
Carrer del Comerç

Metro
Barceloneta (L4)

Mercat de Sant Antoni   G 4

The Mercat de Sant Antoni at the south-western edge of the Barri Xino (see entry) is one of the largest market halls in Barcelona still in active use. The steel-skeleton building (1872–82) by Antoni Rovira i Trias occupies the area of a complete block of streets and the market offers an extremely large choice of fruit, vegetables, fish and seafood.
Around the outside of the building are stalls selling textiles, books, records, coins, stamps, etc.

Location
Ronda de Sant Pau/Ronda de Sant Antoni

Metro
Universitat (L1), Paral.lel (L3)

*Mercat de Sant Josep (Mercat de la Boqueria)   J 4 · b 3

On the south-west side of the Rambla dels Flors (Rambla de Sant Josep; see Ramblas), where in the morning the colourful flower market is held, and directly next to the Palau de la Virreina (see entry) is the large Mercat de Sant Josep (also called the Mercat de la Boqueria), the oldest and most important market hall in Barcelona and the one which is most worth visiting. It was opened in 1840 and offers an impressive and colourful range of goods including fruit, vegetables, meat, regional sausages. In the centre of the hall is the fish market. At other stalls snacks can be obtained.

Location
Rambla de Sant Josep

Metro
Liceu (L3)

Opening out in front of the market hall is the Pla de l'Os, which forms part of the Ramblas. The name means "Bear Square" and even today gipsies occasionally can be seen with their dancing bears. In the street paving is a ground mosaic (1976) by Joan Miró. Opposite lies a rather irreverently flamboyant building with an umbrella and a large Chinese dragon forming part of the façade.

Pla de l'Os

**Montjuïc C 2–G 3

Location south-
west of the old city

Metro Paral.lel (L3);
continue
by funicular and
cable car.

On the southern side of the city and sloping steeply down to the sea rises Montjuïc (213m/700ft). Crowned by a fortress built on its summit, it is the most extensive and most frequented recreational area within the city boundaries and repays an extended visit not just for its scenic beauty with its rich vegetation and large parks, but also because of its museums and amusement park.

**Harbour cable
car (Teleféric)

From the port (see entry) the visitor can travel by cable car (Transbordador Aerí) to the Parc de Miramar, about halfway up the north-eastern side of the hill.

Funicular

From the Avinguda del Paral.lel, which connects the port with the Plaça d'Espanya (see entry), next to the Paral.lel metro station, there is a beach cable railway, running initially underground, up to the Avinguda de Mira-mar, which runs halfway up the side of Montjuïc. Near the upper station is the large municipal open-air swimming-pool.

A chairlift (operating times: June–Sept. Mon.–Fri. noon–8.30pm, Sat., Sun. and public holidays 11am–2.45pm and 4–7.30pm; Sept.–June, except Christmas holidays, daily 11am–2.45pm and 4.30–7pm) provides a continuation up to the castle and offers visitors an even better view, especially across the harbour basin, which is, as already mentioned, spanned by the cable railway. From the intermediate station the visitor can reach the amusement park directly. The chairlift ends immediately next to the castle at the top and there is a restaurant which enjoys an excellent vantage point.

Crustaceans in the Mercat de Sant Josep

*Castell de Montjuïc

The whole of the summit area of Montjuïc is occupied by the extensive buildings and grounds which make up the Castell de Montjuïc (fortress). From the corner bastions in particular, the visitor has a panoramic view across the whole of the metropolis. On the west side stands an ornate memorial to Francisco Franco, which is gradually becoming dilapidated and in the moat there is an archery ground. In the whole fortress site there are several large-calibre guns which command the whole of the port area.

It is well worth taking a walk round the flat roof of the citadel (entrance through the Museu Militar; see below). From there there is a complete panorama over the sea, port, city and mountains.

Museu Militar

The Museu Militar (military museum) is located inside the citadel which is normally open until 9pm In the courtyard stand flat- and sloping-fire guns from the 19th and early 20th c. The exhibition is housed in the rooms surrounding the courtyard and in the casemates.

Open
Tues.–Sat.
10am–2pm,
3.30–8pm; Sun.
and public
holidays
10am–8pm (7pm
Oct–Mar.);
Closed Mon.

From the gateway, where the ticket office is located, the visitor turns left and views the exhibition in a clockwise direction. The library (Rooms 3 and 4) can be visited by prior arrangement. From there we go downstairs into the casemates (Rooms 1–7; photography is forbidden here). In the smaller room on the left and in the neighbouring rooms can be seen displays of blank weapons, firearms, models of battleships and fighting planes, a large model of Montjuïc, as well as models of other Spanish castles, landscape dioramas of historic battlegrounds. On the wall there is a large map showing the individual comarques (districts) and important castles of Catalonia, and a collection of tin soldiers. In the large room (at the bottom of the stairs

View over the city from Castell de Montjuïc

Military souvenirs in the inner courtyard

on the right) there are medieval and more recent weapons (crossbows, flails, armour, blank weapons and firearms).

The tour then returns to the courtyard; here are the auditorium (Room 6) and newly furnished rooms (Room 7 onwards). These contain more historical weapons, extensive collections of modern firearms (handguns from various sources, automatic weapons) and uniforms of various military units. Non-military material is to be found in Room 18, where items connected with the history of the mountain and finds from the old Jewish cemetery can be seen.

From the inner courtyard visitors can go up to the large roof terrace, from which there are splendid views (see above).

Parc d'Atraccions

Open
Daily (except Mon.) in high season; other times Sat., Sun. and public holidays.

Montjuïc is famous above all for the amusement park (Parc d'Atraccions) on its north-eastern slope. There are large car-parks available near the entrances. The park is basically a large permanent fairground with 40 rides, including a big wheel, roller coasters and other similar rides (ghost train, bumper cars); plus an open-air theatre, amusement arcades and a restaurant.
A similar amusement park is located on Tibidabo (see entry).

Mirador del Alcalde

Further down from the amusement park we come to the Mirador del Alcalde with its fountains and superb view across the inner city area and the harbour. The paving in the pedestrian area is very unusual, consisting of concrete pipes, necks and bases from bottles, transmission chains, etc., all decoratively arranged.

Castell de Montjuïc

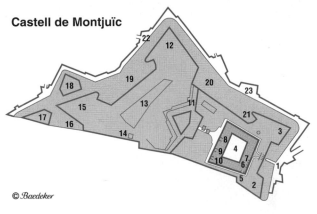

© Baedeker

1	Bridge	12 Velasco Bulwark
2	Sant Carles Bastion	13 Water reservoir
3	Santa Amalia Bastion	14 Transformer station
4	Plaça de Armes	15 Lengua Serpe Bastion
5	Museum entrance	16 Secret door
6	Library	17 Outwork facing the sea
7	Picture gallery	18 Outwork facing the land
8	Toilets	19 Moat
9	Weapons of the Spanish	20 Archery ground
	Army	21 Secret door
10	Spanish armed forces 1981	22 Battlement walk
11	Santa Elena Moat	23 Battlement walk

Jardins de Mossèn Jacint Verdaguer

To the west of the amusement park, stretching downhill to the Plaça Dante and the lower station of the chairlift are the Jardins de Mossèn Jacint Verdaguer, named after the famous Catalan poet (1845–1902). The largest part of the gardens is made up of water terraces on either side of the steps which are covered with water-lilies. An inscription stone bears the words of a poem by Verdaguer.

*Jardins de Mossèn Costa i Llobera

The steep slope of Montjuïc which faces the sea is occupied by the extensive Jardins de Mossèn Costa i Llobera (named after the poet Miquel Costa i Llobera who was a contemporary of Verdaguer). They are reached from the Plaça Dante by crossing the Avinguda de Miramar.

Near the upper station of the port cable railway lies the Plaça de l'Armada, from where there is a good view of the harbour and the old part of the city. In the small adjoining Jardins de Miramar is a statue of a woman by Josep Clarà.

Plaça de l'Armada

Right by the square is the upper entrance to the Jardins de Mossèn Costa i Llobera. This park is very well set out and is famous for its large stocks of succulents, cacti and euphorbias. On a platform there is the bronze statue of a lacemaker by the sculptor Josep Viladomat.

The visitor goes back to the Plaça Dante, passing the Fundació Joan Miró (see entry). In the western part of Montjuïc are to be found part of the sports facilities which are being substantially enlarged for the Olympic Games

Statues . . .

. . . on Montjuïc

(see Olympic Sites), the Museu Arqueològic (see entry), the Museu Etno-lògic (see entry), the Palau Nacional (see entry), the Botanical Gardens (see entry), the Poble Espanyol (see entry), and the new Mercat de les Flors (a theatre converted from a flower market).

Montseny   outside the area of the city plan

The massif of Montseny lies almost 50km/31 miles to the north-east of Barcelona and 30km/19 miles inland from the Costa Daurada. This mountainous area is where the Riu Tordera has its source.

Location
50km/31 miles to
the north-east

*Landscape

The Serra de Montseny is a low mountain range almost completely covered by forest. At the Turó del Home it reaches 1712m/5617ft and this represents the highest point in the Catalan coastal range. Important sources of income are forestry and agriculture; tourism also plays a role, for the national park which lies within the area is very popular for walking and recreation.

From Sant Celoni, situated in the valley of the Riu Tordera, a very winding but extremely scenic road with fine views across to Santa Fe del Montseny (Altitude: 1100m/3609ft), the most important locality within the national park. The village has grown up around a former abbey and today forms a good base for mountain walking. To the west rises the Turó del Home, the summit of which offers superb views in all directions and is the site of a meteorological station.

Santa Fe

◄ *Amusement Park on Montjuïc*

71

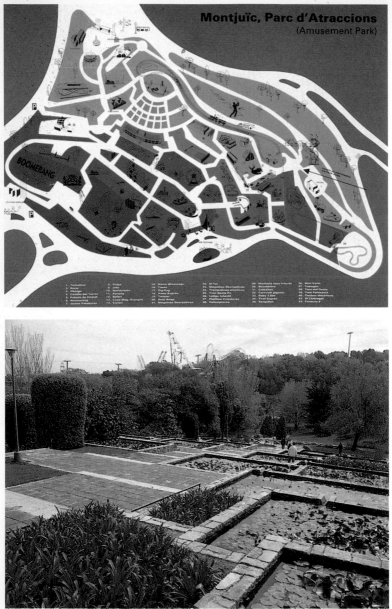

Montjuïc, Parc d'Atraccions
(Amusement Park)

BOOMERANG

1. Terbolino
2. Saxor
3. Vikingo
4. Castillo del Terror
5. Palacio de Cristal
6. Nautionline
6. Jaulas Voladoras
9. Pulpo
9. Jets
10. Nautionline
11. Formula
12. Safari
13. Casa Mag. Espejos
14. Ciclón
15. Barco Miscrosip-
16. Topes
17. Zig-Zag
18. Amor Exprés
19. Twister
20. Hula Hoop
21. Maquinas Recreativas
22. El Tar
23. Máquinas Recreativas
24. Trampolines elásticos
25. Tren Santa Fe
26. Lutiga Infantil
27. Platillos Voladores
28. Helicopteros
29. Montaña rusa infantil
30. Secaderno
31. Cabañas
32. Carrusel gigante
33. Baby 2000
34. Tirol Exprés
35. Gangolles
36. Mini Karts
37. Tobogán
38. Tren del Oesle
39. Tren Fantasma
40. Coches eléctricos
41. El Llobregat
42. Fórmula E

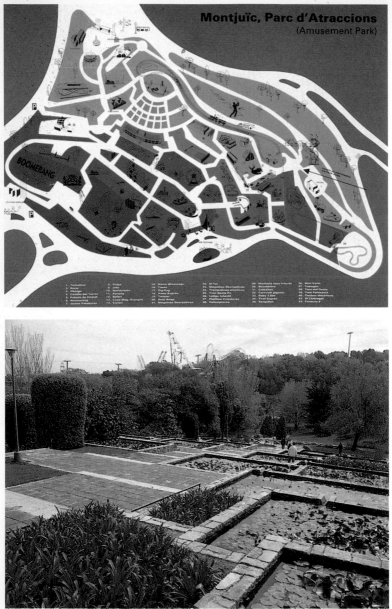

Water terraces in the Jardins de Mossèn Jacint Verdaguer

Cacti and succulents in the Jardins de Mossèn Costa i Llobera

Montserrat   outside the area of the city plan

Montserrat, famed for its monastery, rises some 1220m/4000ft above the plain to the north-west of Barcelona. The visitor wishing to drive from Barcelona to Montserrat is advised to leave the city centre on the Avinguda de la Diagonal in a south-west direction and soon this road merges with the motorway to Martorell. From Martorell follow the main road which goes via Olesa to Monistrol. A short way beyond Olesa a bridge across the valley leads to the cableway (large sign "Aerí"; officially Funicular Aerí del Montserrat) the upper station of which is situated right by the monastery on the mountain. There is also a direct rail line from Barcelona to the cableway, leaving from the station beneath the Plaça d'Espanya. (A combined train, cable car and funicular ticket is available, and there are organised half-day coach tours.)

Location
50km/31 miles to the north-west

The road up to Montserrat (8km/5 miles; at times very steep but well engineered) branches off the main road in Monistrol and winds up the mountain offering fine views of the surrounding country. The road ends at the monastery where there is a large car park.

Access

Montserrat was at one time erroneously thought to be the Monsalvatsch in Wolfram von Eschenbach's saga of the Holy Grail. It is now considered much more likely that the latter is to be found at Salvatierra, a place of pilgrimage on the southern side of the Pyrenees. According to legend the monastery was founded in the year 880 in honour of a wonder-working statue of the Virgin Mary; the first documentary mention dates from 888. In 976 it was handed over to the Benedictine order and in 1025 was considerably enlarged by monks from the Catalan towns of Ripoll and Vich. In 1409 Pope Benedict XIII raised it to the status of an independent abbey and towards the end of the century the monastery printing-house was installed.

History

73

A former monk of Montserrat travelled with Columbus's fleet to the New World in 1493 and he is reputed to have named the island of Montserrat, which forms part of the Lesser Antilles (and is today a British crown colony). In 1522 Ignatius Loyola, who later was to found the Jesuit order, spent some time in the monastery. At the beginning of the 19th c. Napoleon's troops forced their way into Spain; the enormous riches of the monastery became lost during the War of Liberation (from 1808 onwards) and the convent was destroyed in 1811 by the French. More severe losses were brought about by the closure of the monastery during the Carlist Wars (1835–60). The monastery still has its associated school of sacred music ("Escolania"), founded in the 15th c. It is the custom for its youthful members to sing the Salve at the time of Ave Maria (1pm) and also at vespers. The main festivals of Montserrat are on 27 April and 8 September.

**Landscape

Montserrat ("sawn mountain"), the Montsagrat (sacred mountain) of the Catalans, is one of the greatest attractions for visitors in the whole of Spain, both for its scenery and for its famous monastery. It is a massive conglomerate 10km/6 miles long and 5km/3 miles wide, which towers up out of the Catalan plateau, in an almost isolated position across the right bank of the Riu Llobregat and sloping steeply downwards on all sides. With its fantastic rock images formed by erosion it looks from a distance like a huge castle. The highest point in the massif is the 1241m/4073ft mountain Sant Jeroni. From the south-east the mountain is bisected by a huge cleft in the rocks known as the "Vall Malalt" (= evil valley). The monastery stands at its beginning on an outcrop at an altitude of 725m/2379ft. The north-east slope is covered by pine woods, the other sides and the summit by evergreen bushes. The famous flora of the mountain (there are some 1500 plant varieties) was largely destroyed in 1986 by fires.

*Monastery

Open
Daily 6am–8pm

The monastery with its basilica and neighbouring buildings virtually forms a small self-contained town in itself. The road ends at the large car park. Here the visitor has access to an extensive observation terrace on which stands a modern monument to the Catalan poet and mystic, Ramon Llull (Latinised: Raimondus Lullus; 1232–1316), who was born in Palma de Mallorca. The eight steps of the monument resemble a spiral staircase and are called the "steps of knowledge" (stone, fire, plants, animals, human beings, angels, God). Close by stands a circular memorial to the dead.

The inner part of the monastery complex is reached by crossing the Plaça de la Creu ("square of the cross", named after the sculpture of a cross dating from 1927 on the left-hand side). Around the square are souvenir shops, a restaurant, post-office, telephone kiosks and an exchange office. Audio-visual information about Montserrat is available every 30 minutes at the bottom of the steps. On the Plaça de l'Abat Oliba, near the main entrance to the monastery, farmers's wives from the outlying villages sell their produce.

Museu de
Montserrat
Open
Daily 10.30am–2pm
and 3–6pm

From here the visitor enters a broad square, the Plaça de Santa Maria. To the right of the wide central avenue leading to the basilica is the entrance to the new section of the museum, which is situated beneath the square. (A ticket is valid for both sections of the museum). This section contains works by Catalan painters of the 19th and 20th c. and is mainly of regional interest. The old section is to be found diagonally left of the main façade of the church and contains a small Egyptian collection (several copies of well-known large sculptures, small terracottas, seals, a human mummy and two sarcophagi). There are also finds from the Neolithic period, Roman and

Montserrat, the legendary mountain ▶

Montserrat

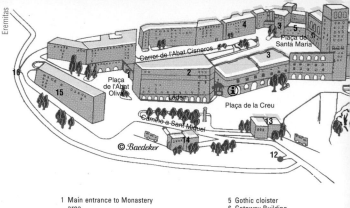

1 Main entrance to Monastery
area
2 Audiovisual Information
3 Museum in two buildings
4 Hotel

5 Gothic cloister
6 Gateway Building
7 Basilica
8 Song School
(Escolania)

Byzantine ceramics and ornaments, coins, antique glasses, Jewish objects of worship (tallit = prayer coat, schofare = ram's horns for ritual use, tora = scrolls).
Further to the left, below the rock, is the Hostal Abad Cisneros (hotel).

Basilica

At the end of the square stands a gatehouse, with five arches in its lower part, three in the upper. It was built between 1942 and 1968 and marks the boundary of the actual area of the church. The reliefs in the three upper arches show (from the left) St Benedict, the Assumption of Mary (according to the dogma of Pope Pius XII) and St George, the patron saint of Catalonia. From time to time groups of pilgrims from Catalonia gather to dance the sardana, a national folk dance. To the left of the façade can be seen the remains of the former Gothic cloister (15th c.).

Between the gatehouse and the actual church there is a fairly narrow inner courtyard with a statue of St Benedict (1927) and next to it the gateway to the monastery (not open to the public). The decorative graffiti on the side façades are modern. The baptistry, which is situated inside the gatehouse building, also opens out onto the inner courtyard. Its entrance is surrounded by decorative 20th c. reliefs.

The basilica, which contains the highly revered statue of the Madonna, dates from the 18th c. but was substantially altered and rebuilt during the 19th and 20th c. The façade shows Renaissance forms, although the figures of Christ and the apostles were only added in 1900.

There are two entrances into the church: the main entrance leads into the nave, while the right-hand side door gives direct access to the Madonna (one way only).
The nave inside is 68m/74yds long, 21m/23yds wide and 33m/67ft high; it is dimly lit by large numbers of votive candles. The interior decoration is modern (19th–20th c.).

Madonna of Monserrat

The Madonna of Montserrat, the "Santa Imatge" of the Catalans, is one of the most important objects of pilgrimage in the whole of Spain. As is frequently the case in Spanish churches, it stands high up behind the high altar and is reached by steps leading from the transept. The staircases are

Montserrat

9 Monument to Ramon Llul
10 Restaurant
11 Cableway Lower Station
   (Funicular Aerí)
12 Monument to Pau (Pablo) Casals

13 Funicular to the Sacred Grotto
   (Cova Santa)
14 Funicular to Sant Joan
15 Gendarmerie (Guarda Civil)
16 Via Crucis (Way of the Cross)

framed by beaten silver ornamentation. The coloured wooden sculpture dates from the 12th or 13th c; the face and hands have become darkened with age and for this reason the figure is called "la Moreneta" (the brown lady). Legend has it that the sculpture is the work of St Luke, who was brought to Spain by St Peter. (The chapel containing "la Moreneta" may be visited daily 8–10.30am, noon–1.30pm and 3–6.30pm.)

The visitor leaves the church by the left transept. Outside on the wall of the rock there are many votive gifts (including wax limbs as thanks for healing) and offertory candles as well as the sacred spring ("Mística Font de l'Aigua de la Vida" and near it a coloured majolica statue of the Mother of God.

The Plaça del Abat Oliva is the beginning of the Via Crucis (Way of the Cross). The fourteen large groups of statues date from between 1904 and 1919 and were restored after the Civil War. At the end of the Stations of the Cross is a chapel (Verge de la Solitud); from the fourteenth station a path leads to the Ermita Sant Miquel (19th c.), the original building of which existed in the 10th c.

Way of the Cross

From the Plaça de la Creu there is a path passing the upper station of the cableway (see page 73) which leads to the Cova Santa with its 17th c. chapel. It is said that the Madonna of Montserrat was kept hidden here during the period of the Moorish occupation and was rediscovered by shepherds.

Cova Santa

At the Plaça de la Creu is the valley station of the cableway leading to Sant Joan. Nearby on the path stands a monument to the Catalan cellist Pau Casals (1876–1973). Sant Joan is one of the thirteen hermitages that once existed in the area of Montserrat; from the upper station there is a beautiful view of the monastery.

Sant Joan

A cableway 680m/744yds long with a 535m/1755ft height difference (the oldest one in Spain) leads from the Manresa road up to the Capilla de Sant Jeroni, from where it is a five-minute walk to the summit of Sant Jeroni, which at 1241m/4073ft is the highest point in the massif.

**Sant Jeroni

77

Monument to Raimundus Lullus . . .   *. . . and one to Pau Casals*

Museu Arqueològic   F 4

Location
Passeig Santa
Madrona

Metro
Poble Espanya
(L1, L3)

Open Tue.–Sat.
9.30am–1pm,
4–7pm, Sun. and
public holidays
10am–2pm Closed
Mon.

Close to the south-eastern edge of the exhibition grounds (see entry) and at the foot of Montjuïc (see entry) is the Museu Arqueològic de Barcelona (Archaeological Museum). This pseudo-Classical circular brick building was originally built as the "Palau d'Arts Gràfiques" for the World Exhibition of 1929 and in 1932 it was enlarged and converted to its present use. The museum's exhibits have their origin in a collection dating back to 1888, which after 1932 was able to be considerably increased through the acquisition of numerous additional items. Today the museum belongs to the Institut de Prehistòria i Arqueologia de la Diputació de Barcelona.

The tour of the museum is devised chronologically and begins with the anthropological development of man (flint tools, a large diorama with the reproduction of an inhabited Stone Age cave). Exhibits from the New Stone Age include ceramics with ribboned and striped decorations. Megalithic culture is represented by carved models from stone graves. Reproductions of graves from the Bronze Age (El Argar culture) follow on, together with urnfield culture and early metal weapons.

Tour

The next section (at present undergoing alteration) is devoted to the Balearic Islands (Balearic cave culture, Talayot culture). A large model depicts the Greek city of Empúries (on the Costa Brava in what is today the province of Girona) and there is a rich collection of finds from the Magna Graecia (Attic and Etruscan vessels), Terra Sigilata and small bronzes.

The rotunda which follows is fashioned in the style of Roman antiquity and decorated with wall paintings; in the display cabinets are a collection of glasses, small items of ceramic work and altar stones.

The tour of the museum at present finishes with the early Christian era and West Gothic culture.

Directly beyond the road leading up to Montjuïc is the Teatre Grec (Greek Theatre) situated in an abandoned quarry on the slope of the mountain. It was designed for the 1929 World Exhibition, using Epidauros as a model – albeit on a much smaller scale. Concentrically arranged rows of seats surround the deep stage, which even today is used for perfomances (Greek classics, etc.).

Teatre Grec

The theatre is surrounded by the Baroque-influenced Jardí Amargs.

To the west opposite the Museum stands the building of the former Mercat dels Flors (Flower market) now a Theatre.

Mercat dels Flors

The "Greek Theatre", based on an ancient design

Museu Clarà   G 9

Location
Carrer Calatrava
27–29

Railway station
(Ferrocarrils de la
Generalitat)
Tres Torres

Open
Tue.–Sun.
9.am–2pm;
Closed Mon.

The Museu Clarà is situated in the select residential area of Sant Gervasi. The sculptor Josep Clarà (1889–1958) occupied the small property until his death; in 1969 the museum, which contains the most important examples of his work, was opened.

The exhibits most worth seeing are the sculptures (statues, etc.), and also the paintings and graphics. A small section is devoted to souvenirs from his personal belongings and works by artists who had close ties of friendship with him. In the small garden are two marble blocks which form part of the artist's legacy and on which lines by the poet Joan Maragall have been chiselled.

Museu d'Art de Catalunya

See Palau Nacional

Museu d'Art Modern   L 3

Location
Parc de la
Ciutadella

Metro
Arc de Triomf (L1)

Open
Mon. 3–7pm;
Tue.–Sat.
9am–7.30pm;
Sun. and public
holidays
9am–1.30pm

The Museum of Modern Art has since 1945 been housed in the extreme left wing of the Palau de la Ciutadella where the Parliament of Catalonia (regional parliament) is also situated. The Municipal Palace was built in the 18th c. as an arsenal, the museum wing being added about the turn of the century.

The term "Museum of Modern Art" is somewhat misleading, for the exhibits – predominantly works by Catalan artists – go back in time via Historicism to the Romantic period. Correspondingly, in the older sections, most of which are arranged in chronological order, the themes are conventional (portraits, genre scenes, landscapes, a few large historical paintings). Of interest is the Art Nouveau section (furniture, pictures, sculpture), and also Expressionist and early modern works and sculptures from the first third of the 20th c.
The visitor then goes up a staircase to the upper floor and here can be seen a graphic collection with a large number of extremely wicked caricatures. The Contemporary Art section, occupying a relatively small area, also displays works by the Catalan artists Joan Miró and Salvador Dalí.
In future the stock of this section is to be moved to the Casa de la Caritat (see entry).
In all the museum provides a representative but fairly restrictive survey of Spanish art (especially Catalan) since about 1830 but is of interest more from the standpoint of art history and less in a general sense.

Museu d'Arts Decoratives   D 9

Location
Palau de Pedralbes

Metro
Palau Reial (L3)

Temporarily closed

The exhibits of the Museu d'Arts Decoratives (Museum of Arts and Crafts) are at present stored in the Palau de Pedralbes (see entry), as the Palau de la Virreina (see entry) where the museum was previously housed is undergoing extensive alterations. The exhibits are only open to view Monday to Friday 10am–1pm by prior arrangement.

The most important part of the collection consists of furniture from the late Gothic period, glassware from the Roman period and gold work from the 15th c.

Museu d'Arts, Indústries i Tradicions Populars

See Poble Espanyol

Museu d'Autòmats

See Tibidabo

*Museu de Cera

J 3 · b 1

The Museu de Cera (Wax Museum) is located at the port end of the Ramblas (see entry) in a rather old-fashioned 19th c. building. The founder of the museum, Enrique Alarcón, a great cineast, has created an eerily beautiful display by means of regularly changing groups of more than 300 wax figures in all, although the characters represented are identifiable less by their physiognomic similarity than by their clothing and general atmosphere.

The visitor reaches the museum through a small inner courtyard and then turns right (where the ticket-office is situated) into an annexe which houses the "Expo-Museum", containing exclusively figures from Hollywood film history.

The main part of the museum is in the building with the high façade which encloses the inner courtyard. This building, largely unrestored and decorated inside with wall and ceiling paintings, gives a good impression of the architecture of the early Modernist period. The tour of the museum begins on the first floor where a double representation of Pope John Paul II greets the visitor. This is followed by large groups of artistic and political figures of past times (incl. Pau Casals, Andrés Segovia, the Shah of Persia, George Sand and Frédéric Chopin), fairy tale characters, and dictators such as Francisco Franco, Adolf Hitler, Mussolini and Mao Tse-Tung. The world of opera is represented by Richard Wagner, Ludwig von Beethoven, Plácido Domingo, Maria Callas and others (with an appropriate sound background). Then follow artists (Francisco Goya and Maja, Pablo Picasso, Joan Miró, Diego Velázquez, Salvador Dalí) and writers (William Shakespeare, Miguel de Cervantes, Pedro Calderón, Jean-Baptiste Molière, etc. and behind them Don Quixote, Sancho Panza and Dulcinea).

Scientists and artists from the turn of the century are gathered together in a coffee-house atmosphere.

On the second floor there is a group of film stars, assembled on the swaying deck of an ocean liner, rulers and knights from the late Middle Ages and the Renaissance period, as well as famous sports personalities. A lift brings the visitor down to the ground floor and the "Viaje Ficción" section ("Fantastic journey"). By means of a deep-sea diving bell and an underwater tunnel the visitor reaches a fantasy world (between the decks on a sailing ship, dripstone cave with Stone Age men, space journey and science fiction monster). On the far side of the souvenir kiosk is the "Terror" section (Alfred Hitchcock; various forms of execution; Bonnie and Clyde in the bank safe). The final exhibit is the "Horror" cabinet with Frankenstein, Dracula and Dr Mabuse.

Location
Passatge de la Banca 7

Metro
Drassanes (L3)

Open
Summer: daily 10am–8pm;
Winter: Mon.–Fri. 10am–1.30pm and 4.30–7.30pm;
Sat., Sun. and public holidays 10am–8pm

Photography forbidden

**Museu de Ceràmica

D 9

The Museu de Ceràmica (Ceramic Museum), housed for a long time in the Palau Nacional (see entry), was recently moved to the Palau de Pedralbes (see entry). At the end of the 19th c. the city made a number of gifts to the

Location
Palau de Pedralbes

Museu de Ceràmica; art in tiles

Metro
Palau Reial (L3)

Open
Tue.–Sun.
9am–2pm;
Closed Mon. and
public holidays

museum, and these formed the nucleus of the collection; in 1931 its own
museum was built. As clay is one of the most frequently used materials,
both in ancient times and nowadays, and fired pottery is moreover
extremely durable, the museum is able to offer an excellent insight into
cultural history as well as providing aesthetically pleasing exhibits. The
latter are divided according to individual Spanish manufacturers as well as
being in chronological order, and the whole blends in well with the back-
cloth of palace and gardens.

The Historical Department can be found on the first floor of the palace.
In Room 1 are ceramics from the Islamic-Spanish culture group.
Rooms 2–5 house a large number of pieces manufactured in Valencia up to
the 18th c. (strong Moorish influence; some in metallic-effect glaze). Room
3 also contains monochrome blue tiles, some with graphic decoration
(animals and human beings), religious symbols, coats-of-arms and guild-
marks; Room 5 also has some examples of glazing to produce a metallic
effect.
Room 6 contains works from Talavera de la Reina (now the province of
Toledo) and Puente del Arzobispo, dating from the Renaissance to the
19th c. The decoration is partly blue monochrome, partly multi-coloured
(animals, human beings, scenes from everyday life).
Pieces from the ceramic centres of Aragón (from the 13th c. onwards) are
displayed in Rooms 7 and 8. Room 7 contains partly monochrome, partly
green and blue china; on the wall will be found a description of the
technique used to achieve the colour effect (green being copper oxide,

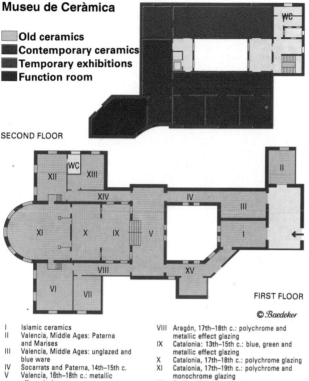

Museu de Ceràmica

☐ **Old ceramics**
■ **Contemporary ceramics**
■ **Temporary exhibitions**
■ **Function room**

SECOND FLOOR

FIRST FLOOR

© Baedeker

I	Islamic ceramics
II	Valencia, Middle Ages: Paterna and Marises
III	Valencia, Middle Ages: unglazed and blue ware
IV	Socarrats and Paterna, 14th–15th c.
V	Valencia, 16th–18th c.: metallic effect glazing
VI	Talavera de la Reina and Puente del Arzobispo, 16th–19th c.
VII	Araagón, 16th–18th c.: Terol
VIII	Aragón, 17th–18th c.: polychrome and metallic effect glazing
IX	Catalonia: 13th–15th c.: blue, green and metallic effect glazing
X	Catalonia, 17th–18th c.: polychrome glazing
XI	Catalonia, 17th–19th c.: polychrome and monochrome glazing
XII	Seville, 16th–18th c.
XIII	L'Alcora, 18th–19th c.
XIV	L'Alcora, 18th–19th c.
XV	Valencia, 18th–19th c.

brown manganese oxide and blue cobalt compounds). Room 8 houses monochrome and blue-green vessels, some with subjective, some with purely ornamental motifs; a display cabinet on the wall contains various stoops.

From Catalonia, always the producer of important ceramics, come the items displayed in Rooms 9–11. In Room 10 are polychrome table-ware and decorative china; particularly impressive are the two large pictures in glazed tiles depicting a bull-fight and a banquet in a large middle-class house. The semi-circular Room 11 is noted for its display of glazed tiles showing skilled craftsmen at work as well as animal and everyday scenes. The Islamic tradition lingered long in Seville in particular, even until the Renaissance (Room 12). In the glass display cabinets on the walls can be seen some long friezes portraying a complete historical story.

In Alcora (now the province of Castellón de la Plana) a new factory was built in 1727 to manufacture European-type goods (Rooms 13 and 14).

Polychrome china from Valencia (19th c.), predominantly the popular decorated tiles known as "azulejos" (from the Arabic "az-zuleyche" = mosaic, not – as once assumed – from the Spanish "azul", meaning blue), is exhibited in Room 15.

On the second floor will be found the Department of Contemporary Ceramic Art, some with traditional and epigonic (more modern) decoration based on old patterns, but mainly avant-garde. The spacious cabinets in the last room contain works by Joan Miró and Pablo Picasso. Temporary exhibitions are also held on this floor.

The museum also possesses an Educational Department, a ceramic workshop and a specialist library (open 10am–1pm).

Museu de Geologia (Museu Martorell)   L 3 · d 2

Location
Parc de la
Ciutadella

Metro
Arc de Triomf (L1)

Open
Tue.–Sun.
9am–2pm;
Closed Mon.

The museums in the Parc de la Ciutadella (see entry) include the Museu de Geologia (Geological Museum; also known as the Museu Martorell, after its founder). It is linked with the Institute of Natural Sciences. Opened in 1882, it is housed in a low Neo-Classical building which was built for the 1888 World Exhibition, and is the first museum building in Barcelona which was intended to be used as such from the outset.

The entrance is in the gabled central section of the side facing the park. In the rooms to the left of the entrance hall can be seen minerals, mainly precious and semi-precious stones (including copies in rock-crystal of the largest known diamonds) as well as exhibits showing the technical applications of precious and non-ferrous metals. Basically, the minerals are arranged according to their chemical structure.
At the end of the hall, distinguishable by the light shining through the agate panes, is a darkened room with minerals bathed in long and short-wave ultra-violet light, producing interesting luminous effects.

Museu de la Ciència

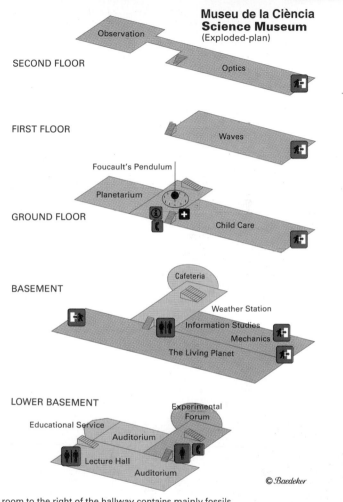

Museu de la Ciència
Science Museum
(Exploded-plan)

SECOND FLOOR — Observation, Optics

FIRST FLOOR — Waves

GROUND FLOOR — Planetarium, Foucault's Pendulum, Child Care

BASEMENT — Cafeteria, Weather Station, Information Studies, Mechanics, The Living Planet

LOWER BASEMENT — Experimental Forum, Educational Service, Auditorium, Lecture Hall, Auditorium

© Baedeker

The room to the right of the hallway contains mainly fossils.

Next to the Geological Museum stands the Palm House with its exotic flora.   Palm House

Museu de la Catedral

See Cathedral

Museu de la Ciència   J 11

The Museu del Ciència (Science Museum) lies at the foot of Tibidabo (see **Location** entry). It is sponsored by the Caixa de Pensions de Catalunya (Pension   Carrer Roviralta 55

Museu de la Música

**Railway station
(FF.CC.)**
Avinguda del
Tibidabo

Insurance Company of Catalonia), which is also active in other spheres as a supporter of cultural pursuits. The museum building, erected for charitable purposes in the early 20th c., has been suitably extended. Nearby runs the city ring road, constructed specially for the forthcoming Olympic Games and separating the museum from Tibidabo.

Open
Tues.–Sun.
10am–8pm;
Closed Mon.

The aim of the extensive experimental collection is to explain – mainly by means of simple experiments which people can carry out themselves – natural history phenomena and relationships to as wide a spectrum of the populace as possible. The main emphasis is on ecology, optical, accoustic and sensorial awareness, with considerable space devoted to each.

Outside, near the entry kiosk, an old submarine has been put on display, partly opened up so that the interior can be inspected.

The museum is particularly valuable for children of primary school age upwards, not least because of the many opportunities for personal experiments and activities; they should spend at least half a day there. For smaller children there is a play-room (with child minders), equipped with toys on specific themes.

Planetarium

The museum also has a separate Planetarium with a demonstration lasting about half an hour (additional charge; Mon.–Fri. at 1 and 6pm; Sat., Sun. and public holidays every half hour; children under four not admitted). There is another Planetarium (see entry) on the Carrer de les Ecole Pies.

Museu de la Música   K 7

Location
Diagonal 373

Metro
Diagonal (L3, L5)

Open
Tues.–Sun.
9am–2pm;
Closed Mon.

In the Avenida de la Diagonal, which cuts across the Eixample district of the city, near the Plaça de Joan Carles I which forms the junction with the Passeig de Gràcia, lies the Museu de la Música (Music Museum), founded in 1947. The house in which it is contained was built in 1902 by the architect Josep Puig i Cadafalch, and is one of the most important examples of Modernisme (see Introduction, Modernisme) in Barcelona.

The collection is arranged by groups of instruments. Among the string instruments the collection of guitars dating from the 17th c. is one of the most comprehensive in Europe. Attention is also drawn to the collection of instruments played with a bow; there are also dulcimers, harps, lutes, balalaikas and mandolines.
Wind and percussion instruments are exhibited on the floor above. Adjoining is a display of keyboard instruments, including harpsichords and organs.
The museum also contains a collection of music reproduction equipment, a record library and a specialist library. The staff are happy to give advice on technical matters.

Museu de les Arts de l'Espectacle

See Palau Güell

Museu del Futbol Club Barcelona   D 8

Location
Avinguda Arístides
Maillol

A little way to the south-east, adjoining the Zona Universitaria, on land designed to provide Olympic facilities (see Olympic Sites), lies the huge stadium (Camp Nou) of the famous F.C. Barcelona Football Club, with some 125,000 seats, making it one of the largest in the world.

The club, several times national champions and European Cup winners, has its own museum here (via Gate 2 of the entrance pavilion), displaying trophies and historical documents as well as an audiovisual show on several screens.

A good general view of the stadium can be had from the president's box.

Metro
Collblanc (L5)

Open Tues.–Fri.
10am–1pm and
4pm–6pm,
Sat. Sun. and
public holidays
10am–1pm;
Closed Mon.

Museu del Libre i de les Arts Grafiques

See Poble Espanyol

Museu del Perfum   J 5

A private perfume company has its offices on the broad Passeig de Gràcia (see entry), and runs a small specialised museum (open Mon.–Fri. 10am–1.30pm and 4pm–7pm; closed Sat., Sun. and public holidays). This provides an interesting insight into the history of fragrances and scents, including highly artistic antique containers, bottles and the like, from the Baroque period (17th/18th c.) to the present day.

Location
Passeig de Gràcia
39

Metro
Passeig de Gràcia
(L3, L4)

Museu del Temple Expiatori de la Sagrada Família

See Sagrada Família

Museu de Zoologia   L 4 · d 2

The Museu de Zoologia (Zoological Museum) stands at the western end of the Parc de la Ciutadella (see entry). This somewhat unique building in a pseudo-Moorish mixture of styles was erected by Lluís Domènech i Montaner as a gastronomic concern for the 1888 World Exhibition, and is popularly known as the "castell dels tres dragons" ("Three Dragons Castle").
Temporary exhibitions are held on the ground floor, where there is also a comprehensive insect collection and skeletons of a whale and a mammoth. Other glass cabinets contain mussels and snails as well as stuffed birds.
A staircase with an attractive stairwell leads to the upper floor, which houses the major part of the permanent exhibitions. These include a collection of birds' eggs, stuffed mammals (with corresponding skeletons by the side), and preserved molluscs, fish, reptiles and amphibians. At the end of the large main hall, behind a glass door, can be seen a conchological study-collection (mussel and snail shells).
All the collections are used for research and teaching purposes. Although its layout is extremely antiquated the museum is spotlessly clean and orderly and possesses considerable nostalgic charm. It is currently being extended.

Location
Parc de la
Ciutadella

Metro
Arc de Triomf (L1)
Ciutadella (L4)

Open
Tues.–Sun.
9am–2pm;
Closed Mon.

**Museu d'Història de la Ciutat   J 4 . c 2

Tours of the excavations on the second Sunday of every month, and the section dedicated to famous Catalans on the third Sunday of every month.

On the Plaça del Rei stands the Casa Clariana Padellás (originally built nearby in the 15th c. and rebuilt on its present site in 1931), a typical

Location
Plaça del Rei

Metro
Jaume I (L4)

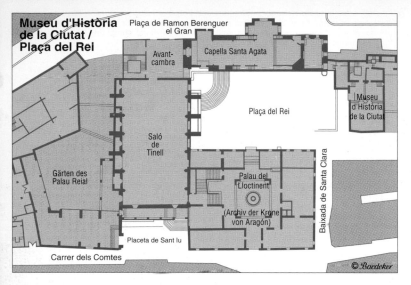

Museu d'Història de la Ciutat / Plaça del Rei

Plaça de Ramon Berenguer el Gran

Avant-cambra

Capella Santa Agata

Plaça del Rei

Museu d'Història de la Ciutat

Saló de Tinell

Gärten des Palau Reial

Palau del Lloctinent

Baixada de Santa Clara

(Arxiv der Krone von Aragón)

Placeta de Sant Iu

Carrer dels Comtes

© Baedeker

Open
Mon. 3.30–8pm,
Tues.–Sat.
9am–8.30pm;
Sun. and public
holidays
9am–1.30pm

Tours

medieval urban palace. Important remains of the old Roman town were discovered when excavating for the foundations on its new site, which led the authorities to decide to make the building an Historical Museum.

The secular church on higher ground and a large room in the former royal palace (see Museu Marés), the Saló de Tinell built in 1370, also belong to the museum. The latter is where Christopher Columbus was received by Their Catholic Majesties on his return from his first voyage to America.

In the basement can be seen the uncovered remains of the Roman town (with excellent printed information provided), as well as models of the excavations in display cabinets. The remains include parts of the heating system, mosaic floors, parts of the surrounding walls and the water and drainage systems. Also of interest is the large oil-mill with big bulbous receptacles in situ. From the cellars visitors can enter a narrow shaft set vertically in the town wall, where they can see how the old Roman hidden passages and the like were blocked up during the Middle Ages.

Then proceed further up the stairs to Rooms 12–16. In the stairwell can be seen a collection of copper pots and pans as well as colourful glazed tiles (everyday scenes, animals and human beings; see also Museu de Ceramica).
In Room 12 a form of family tree shows the various trade-guilds with the names of their patrons.
In Room 13 will be found a number of historical panels. In Room 14 are wooden stamps used for textile printing as well as examples of materials; on the wall hangs a painting, dating from the first half of the 19th c., of a clothing shop in Barcelona.
Room 11 contains a quantity of sketches illustrating the historical development of the city; of particular interest is the large plan for the redevelopment of the Eixample (see entry), by Ildefons Cerdà, signed 7th June 1859, with the original lithograph stones. In Room 10 hang a number of historical paintings.

Placa de Rei, the Royal Square in the Old Town ▶

The stairs then lead up to the second floor which is at present closed; however, the terrace, from which there is an excellent view of the Plaça del Rei, is worth seeing.

The Galeria de Catalans Il.lustres (see entry) in the Carrer del Bisbe Caçador also belongs to the museum.

Punt Zero

The "Barcelona Punt Zero" is a series of guided tours through the historical quarter of the city, beginning at 10am. Detailed information can be obtained and the obligatory advance booking made at the Museum Information Service (Carrer de Verguer 2; tel. 3 15 30 53).

Plaça del Rei

The Plaça del Rei ("King's Square"; not to be confused with the Plaça Reial near the Ramblas – see entry), is one of the most beautiful squares in the old town. It is surrounded by splendid medieval buildings and is open to the narrow streets of the old town only on its southern side. The following description begins from the left of that opening and proceeds clockwise.

Palau del
Lloctinent

The Palau del Lloctinent del Rei ("Palace of the Royal Lieutenant") is a cold, flat building of the mid-16th c., which houses the Arxiu de la Corona d'Aragó (Archives of the Crown of Aragón). The coats-of-arms of the heads of state are repeated several times on the façade. The colourful inner courtyard represents the transition from Gothic to Renaissance.

Saló del Tinell

Opposite the entrance to the Plaça stands the square Romanesque building, the Saló del Tinell (Throne Room), dominated by a rectangular tower in the Tuscan style. The giant hall, spanned by broad, semi-circular arched girders, is of historical importance; it was here that Christopher Columbus, following his first expedition to the New World, was received almost as an equal by the Spanish rulers Ferdinand II and Isabella I (the "Reyes Católicos"). The hall is entered through an ante-room, which is connected with the square by a semi-circular open staircase. Temporary exhibitions are held here from time to time.

Capella Santa
Agata

The Capella Santa Agata, built in the Gothic style on the old Roman town wall, and now a secular building, was once the royal palace chapel. It is also accessible via the above-mentioned open staircase.

The single-naved interior contains a Gothic picture-altar, two Gothic gravestones high up and some priests' cells; the former sacristy has a large iron mechanical clock dating from the year 1576.

The old windows in the choir and gallery show the various coats-of-arms of the counts of Barcelona.

Museu Frederic
Marès

See entry

Plaça de l'Angel

The Plaça de l'Angel is at the junction of Via Laietana and Carrer Jaume I, which leads from the Plaça de Sant Jaume and continues into Carrer de la Princesa. To the right, just off the wide main street leading to the southeast, can be seen remains of the old town wall, on which stands the Palau de Requesens (see Galeria de Catalans Il.lustres).

Museu d'Història de la Medicina de Catalunya   J 6

Location
Passatge Mercader
11

The Museu d'Història de la Medicina de Catalunya (regional museum of medical history) houses in fourteen rooms some 2,500 exhibits illustrative of the principal developments in medical practice, especially in anatomy,

epidemiology, physiology and bacteriology. Special exhibitions can be seen in the basement.
The foundation which supports the museum also conducts specialist events for medical students.
Open: Thur. 10am–1pm. Guided tours: by arrangement.

Metro
Diagonal (L3, L5)

Museu d'Història del Calçat   J 4 · b–c 2

On the little Plaça de Felip Neri, to the south-west near the cathedral, (for location see Barri Gòtic, detailed plan) stands a pretty Renaissance building which was once the headquarters of the municipal shoemakers' guild. It now houses the Museu d'Història del Calçat (History of Footwear Museum) which shows, by means of a large collection of examples, the historical development of shoes and shoe-making mainly in Catalonia. There is also a display of shoes worn by famous people.

Location
Plaça Felip Neri

Metro Jaume I
(L14), Liceu (L3)

Open Tues.–Sun.
11am–2pm; Closed
Mon.

The Plaça Felip Neri was named after the Italian Filippo Neri (1515–95) who was canonised in 1622 and who founded the Order of Oratorians in 1575. The Barcelona congregation (commonly known as "Felipons") was founded towards the end of the 17th c.; the monastery was built in 1673 and remodelled in the 18th c. Typical of the Counter-Reformation, it shows Baroque influence, something of a rarity in Barcelona. The exterior walls have bullet-holes sustained in the Civil War, when a number of Oratorian monks were shot.

Oratorian College

*Museu d'Holografia   J 4 · c2

The Museu d'Holografia (Holographic – and Holoscopic – Museum) is the first of its kind in Spain. This little museum, resembling a gallery, is reached from the Plaça Sant Jaume through the Carrer Jaume I, where the entrance to the first building opens off on the left.

Location
Carrer Jaume I 1

Metro
Jaume I (L4)

Holography is a new achievement in three-dimensional pattern-producing techniques which only became fully practicable following the development of lasers. Objects wrapped in plastic sheets and subjected to interference between a coherent light-beam and light defracted from the same beam by the object produce a solid-looking picture (also in colour). According to the position of the observer and the angle at which the light falls, the foreground and background appear to move closer or further away, various degrees of movement being detectable.

Open
Tues.–Sat. 11am–
1.30pm and
5.30pm–8.30pm;
Closed Sun., Mon.
and public holidays

The impression produced by the hologram set up on the first floor (be careful of the cross-beam in the stairwell!) is truly breathtaking: it may be a confusion of spiral springs and wood-shavings shooting out of the frame, a large flower springing towards the observer or the portrait of a Rocker who suddenly spits large splinters of glass out of his mouth – the illusion (without the need for special spectacles or anything like that) is complete.

On the ground floor there is a large selection of holograms for sale, ranging from cheap plaques to larger items costing thousands of pesetas or more (up to 40 × 50cm/16 × 20in in size).

Museu Diocesà   J 4 · c 2

The Museu Diocesà de Barcelona (Barcelona Diocesan Museum) possesses a collection of religious art, mainly from the diocesan area, including some remarkable Romanesque works.

Location
Carrer Bisbe 5

Metro
Jaume I (L4)

The museum is not open to the general public; specialists in the subject must first present themselves at the Seminari Conciliar (Carrer de la Diputació 231; tel. 2 54 17 56).
Open only to specialists

Museu Etnogràfic Andino-Amazònic   E 10

Location
Carrer Cardenal
Vives i Tutó 2–16

Metro
Maria Christina (L3)

Open
1st Sun. of every
month, noon–2pm;
Closed Aug. and
Sept.

The Museu Etnogràfic Andino-Amazònic (also known as the Museu Etnografico-Missional, i.e. Ethnographic Museum of the Andean and Amazonian Regions) is in the care of the Capuchin order of monks in Catalonia and is housed in their monastery buildings. The small but extremely well cared for and displayed collection is specialised and covers the native cultures in those areas of Latin America where the order has missions.

A monk (he should be addressed as "padre") will guide you through the museum; a knowledge of Spanish will be a great help in understanding him. On display are small works of art, prepared slides and skeletons of Central American animals, a collection of butterflies and insects and also weapons.

On leaving the museum it is customary to make a suitable donation "para el monasterio", i.e. "for the monastery".

Museu Etnològic   F 4

Location
Passeig de Santa
Madrona

Metro
Poble Sec (L3)

Open
Mon. 2–8.30pm,
Tues.–Sat.
9am–8.30pm;
Sun. and
public holidays
9am–2pm

Guided tours
Tues.–Fri.
9am–2pm

The Museu Etnològic (Ethnological Museum) is situated on a bend in the Passeig de Santa Madrona, which leads up from the Exhibition Centre to Montjuïc (see entries). Built in 1973 and specially designed for exhibitions, the building consists of ajacent hexagons, with generous areas of glass providing ideal space for displays.

The emphasis of the collections (which currently comprise over 20,000 items) is on the cultures of Asia, Africa, America and Oceania, covering biological, ethnographic, cultural and social aspects.

The huge stock of exhibits which the museum possesses means that only temporary specialised displays on individual themes can be on display at any one time, so before arranging a visit it is advisable to obtain details of the current subjects covered (tel. 4 24 64 02). The museum also provides an educational service and a specialist library (open Tues.–Sat. 9am–2pm).

There is also a branch of the museum (Museu d'Arts, Indústries i Tradicions Populars) in Poble Espanyol (see entry).

*Museu Frederic Marès   K 4

Location
Plaça Sant Iu 5–6

Metro
Jaume I (L4)

Open
Tue.–Sat. 9am–2pm
and 4pm–7pm;
Sun. and public
holidays 9am–2pm;
Closed Mon.

On display in the museum is the former private collection of the sculptor Frederic Marès Deulovol which was donated to the city; in addition to religious art there is a large department devoted to cultural history from the 15th to early 20th c. from the private library of Marès. The beautiful building in which it has been housed since 1946 forms part of the Salò de Tinell complex (see Museu d'Història de la Ciutat).

Access to the museum is through an archway from the Carrer dels Comtes de Barcelona, leading into a picturesque inner courtyard. The ground floor contains an outstanding collection of Romanesque and Gothic sacred works of art (particularly crucifixes, the Romanesque being most impressive, and a number of pictures believed to have miraculous powers). Adjoining this is a collection of large and small Roman sculptures.

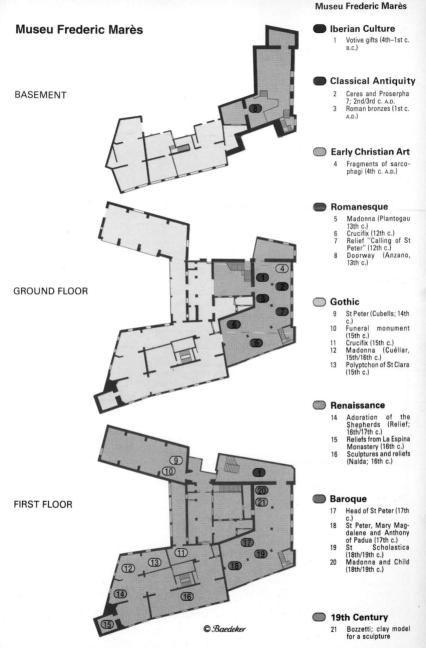

Museu Frederic Marès

BASEMENT

GROUND FLOOR

FIRST FLOOR

© *Baedeker*

Museu Frederic Marès

● **Iberian Culture**
 1 Votive gifts (4th–1st c. B.C.)

● **Classical Antiquity**
 2 Ceres and Proserpha 7; 2nd/3rd c. A.D.
 3 Roman bronzes (1st c. A.D.)

● **Early Christian Art**
 4 Fragments of sarcophagi (4th c. A.D.)

● **Romanesque**
 5 Madonna (Plantogau 13th c.)
 6 Crucifix (12th c.)
 7 Relief "Calling of St Peter" (12th c.)
 8 Doorway (Anzano, 13th c.)

● **Gothic**
 9 St Peter (Cubells; 14th c.)
 10 Funeral monument (15th c.)
 11 Crucifix (15th c.)
 12 Madonna (Cuéllar, 15th/16th c.)
 13 Polyptchon of St Clara (15th c.)

● **Renaissance**
 14 Adoration of the Shepherds (Relief; 16th/17th c.)
 15 Reliefs from La Espina Monastery (16th c.)
 16 Sculptures and reliefs (Nalda; 16th c.)

● **Baroque**
 17 Head of St Peter (17th c.)
 18 St Peter, Mary Magdalene and Anthony of Padua (17th c.)
 19 St Scholastica (18th/19th c.)
 20 Madonna and Child (18th/19th c.)

● **19th Century**
 21 Bozzetti; clay model for a sculpture

93

Museu Frederic Marès

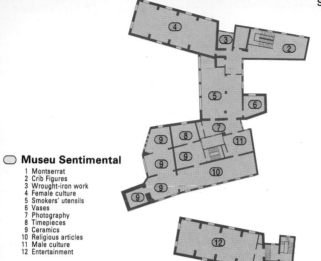

SECOND FLOOR

◯ **Museu Sentimental**

1 Montserrat
2 Crib Figures
3 Wrought-iron work
4 Female culture
5 Smokers' utensils
6 Vases
7 Photography
8 Timepieces
9 Ceramics
10 Religious articles
11 Male culture
12 Entertainment

THIRD FLOOR

© Baedeker

Museu Frederic Marès: "History in Stone"

In the "crypt" is an extensive lapidarium (stone engravings from the Early Christian, Romanesque and Gothic periods); the foundations contain a small part of the Roman town-wall. Note the two Romanesque portals with rounded arches, one still with the original wood-panelled doors. There are also two marble graves from the late 14th and early 15th c.

An open staircase from the inner courtyard leads up to the first floor. Here can be found the second part of the collection of religious sculpture (Gothic, Renaissance, Baroque); a small collection of dolls and dolls' clothes; lace. coins and medals; chests and caskets; Gothic panels and chasubles (vestments worn at Mass).

The second floor houses the "Colleciò Sentimental", a comprehensive collection of small Baroque works of art, tinware, hand-tools and various kinds of scales, playing cards, advertisements, dried flowers under glass, scrap-books, ashtrays, antique cameras, tobacco jars, binoculars, watches, old seals, table silver, porcelain and much more.

Museu i Centre d'Estudis de l'Esport   H 7

The Museu i Centre d'Estudis de l'Esport (sporting museum and study centre) is housed in a building, dating from the Modernistic period, which was used by Dr Melcior Colet as his consulting rooms and private clinic. In 1982 he made it into a foundation which bears his name and which serves the needs of sport and its cultural importance.

Today the museum houses a variety of exhibitions on various sporting themes (mostly with Catalonian connections). In addition it is the headquarters of a scientific sports research institute.

Open: Mon.–Fri. 10am–2pm and 4–8pm.
Closed: Sat., Sun. and public holidays.

Location
Carrer Buenos Aires 56–58

Metro
Hospital Clínic (L5)

**Museu Marítim   H 3 · a 1

Near the port (see entry), west of the Columbus Monument are the striking vaulted buildings with many bays, the form of which clearly betrays their original function. Situated in the docks (Catalan: "Drassanes"), they were once a naval arsenal for the royal fleet. Here has been established the Museu Marítim (maritime museum) which at present is undergoing reorganisation. Therefore the following description may not be entirely accurate. Some of the rooms are reserved for special exhibitions.

The shipyard was first built in the 13th c., and by the 18th c. it had been extended to twelve bays. This is where the galleys of the Crown of Aragón were built, serviced and repaired. However, after the discovery of America maritime interests moved to the Atlantic, the importance of the shipyards fell appreciably, and the buildings became used as storage warehouses, powder magazines and military barracks. In 1936 it was officially decided to set up a museum here. Since 1976 the whole complex has been under a preservation order. On the southern side, on the Avinguda del Parallel, remains of the old town wall have been preserved.

The museum, which is constantly being extended, portrays all aspects of the sea and seafaring by means of ships, models of ships, nautical equipment, tools and weapons, diagrams and drawings. Signs guide the visitor on a circular tour.

The large exhibition hall is dominated by an excellent full-size replica of the galleon "Real". This was the flagship of the fleet which, under the command of Don Juan d'Austria, defeated the Turks on 7 October 1571 off Lepanto (Greek: Naupaktos; south-west Peloponnes) to give Spain mastery of the Mediterranean. The original figurehead, the "Christ of Lepanto", can now be seen in the Cathedral (see entry). The reason for the rebuilding

Location
Plaça Portal de la Pau

Metro
Drassanes (L3)

Open
Tue.–Sat.
10am–2pm and
4pm–7pm;
Sun. and public
holidays
10am–2pm;
Closed Mon.

At present being
reorganised

Museu Marítim: history of seafaring in the old shipyard

which took place from 1960 onwards was the approaching 400th anniversary of that victory.

A large number of explanatory diagrams and drawings show the submarine topography of the globe, characteristic Mediterranean winds and their names in various Mediterranean languages, migration routes taken by the most important of the marine animals, the maritime food-chain, sailors' knots and rigging. Also exhibited are some fishing boats (including one from Málaga painted in typical designs), ships' guns, torpedoes and mines.

Museu Militar de Montjuïc

See Montjuïc

**Museu Picasso

K 3 · c–d 2

On Carrer Montcada, one of the most picturesque of the narrow streets in the old town, stands the Palau Berenguer de Aguilar, an imposing Late Gothic palace which now houses the Picasso Museum. The collections, arranged in chronological order, include paintings and drawings as well as prints (lithographs, etchings) from all of Pablo Picasso's artistic periods. The exhibition rooms begin on the first floor; labelling is in two languages (Catalan and Spanish).

Rooms 1–7 contain his early work, and Rooms 8–10 the graphic collection. The artist's early work is strongly influenced by Naturalism and Impres-

Location
Carrer Montcada
15–19

Metro
Jaume I (L4)

Open
Mon.–Sat.
10am–8pm,
Sun. 10am–3pm
Closed Mon.

◀ *The galleon "Real", flagship of Don Juan of Austria*

Sculpture outside the Maritime Museum, a memorial of the Battle of Lepanto

A drawing by Picasso

sionism. In Room 5 can be found the large-sized painting of "Ciéncia y Caridad", together with his preliminary sketches and studies.

At present being reorganised

On the second floor Rooms 11–14 are at present closed. Rooms 15–17 house the continuation of his graphic works; Rooms 18 onwards show paintings arranged in chronological order, with the beginnings of his Cubist period in Room 19. Room 20 is devoted to the "Meninas", a monochrome paraphrase of the work of the same name by Diego Velázquez together with preliminary sketches. Room 21 displays the polychrome version. In Room 22 you can see variations on the theme "Los Pichones" ("The Doves").

On the ground floor are a cafeteria and a large horizontal window which provides a view of a Roman provisions store, with some large two-handled pots.

*Museu Tèxtil i d'Indumentària

K 3· c–d 2

Opposite the Museu Picasso (see entry) stands a 13th c. palace, now the home of the Museu Tèxtil i d'Indumentària (Textile and Clothing Museum). It possesses items from the 4th c. A.D. onwards, as well as from regions inhabited by the Coptics (Egyptians), Moors and from the Christian West.

Location
Carrer Montcada
12–14

Metro
Jaume I (L4)

The ticket office is in the pretty Renaissance inner courtyard, where there is a small display of dolls' clothes and fashion jewellery. The exhibition rooms begin on the first floor, and by following the signs the exhibits will be seen in chronological order. They include finery and sophisticated clothing from the 16th–18th c. as well as many accessories (shoes, handbags, capes); on the walls hang large tapestries. In Room 11 will be found an extensive group of sumptuous 18th c. garments and a display cabinet with shoes; in Room 12 there are similar items from the Empire and Biedermeier periods. Going up one set of stairs brings the visitor to some temporary exhibitions covering specialised subjects, as well as a weaving-loom and a model of same.

Open
Tues.–Sat.
9am–2pm and
4.30pm–7pm;
Sun. and public
holidays 9am–2pm;
Closed Mon.

A little further along the Carrer Montcada, at No. 20, stands the Palau Dalmases, which has been the headquarters since 1962 of the cultural organisation known as the "Omnium Cultural". The 17th c. palace boasts a beautiful inner courtyard with a Renaissance staircase.

Palau Dalmases

The 15th/16th c. Palau Cervelló, on the opposite side of the street at No. 25, is also worth seeing. It houses the Maeght Art Gallery.

Palau Cervelló

Museu Verdaguer

See Casa-Museu Verdaguer

Olympic Sites

On 25 July 1992 in the Olympic Stadium (see below) the XXVth Modern Summer Olympics will begin. The Organising Committee plans to have four large arenas spread around the city, all within a radius of some five kilometres (three miles). Only very few contests will be held outside the city area. As far as possible, existing stadia and halls will be used, after being completely modernised and extended.

General

Montjuïc

The arenas on Montjuïc and on the Exhibition Grounds (see entries) form the core of the Olympic events: they comprise Anella Olimpíca (Olympic

Ring) encompassing the Olympic Stadium, Palau Sant Jordi and Bernat Picornell Swimming Pools, as well as complementary installations such as the sports university – INEFC (Institut Nacional d'Educadió Fisica de Catalunya), the Fuixarda and Serrahima Stadiums, Palau Municipal d'Esports, Montjuïc Municipal Swimming Pool, Montjuïc Shooting Range and Parc de Migidia.

Area de la Diagonal

Another sports centre is the south-western part of the Avinguda de la Diagonal, near the Zona Universitaria (see University). Here lie the Camp Nou Stadium (see Museu del Futbol Club Barcelona), Palau Blaugrana directly opposite, the adjoining "Miniestadi" (mini-stadium) of the Reial Club de Polo, the Pavelló Municipal del CE Hospitalet Nord and the Sarrià Sports Stadium.

Vall d'Hebron

In the Vall d'Hebron district on the western edge of the city will be found the Velòdrom (cycle racing track), the Palau Municipal d'Esports Vall d'Hebron, the archery range and La Teixonera tennis club.

Parc de Mar

The large Olympic Village (accommodation for 15,000 people), with two blocks of high-rise flats (at 136m/436ft Barcelona's tallest buildings), the Nova Icária Marina, Estacío del Nord (for table tennis) and a hall for badminton, has been newly built on some former industrial land north of the port (see entry).

Site of the Olympic Games (1992) on Montjuïc

Sports arenas outside the city

Other competition sites are to be found at Badalona, Banyoles, Castelldefels, Granollers, L'Hospitalet de Llobregat, La Seu d'Urgell, Reus, Sabadell,
Sant Sadurni d'Anoia, Terrassa, València, Vic, Viladecans and Zaragoza.

Palau Dalmases

See Museu Tèxtil i d'Indumentària

Palau de la Diputaciò

See Palau de la Generalitat

Palau de la Generalitat   J 3 · c 2

Opposite the Casa de la Ciutat (see entry), on the north-western side of the
Plaça de Sant Jaume, the main traffic junction in the Barri Gòtic, towers
the former Palau de la Diputació, built in the 15th c. and once the seat of the
medieval body of provincial representatives. Today it houses the Generalitat de Catalunya, the autonomous government of Catalonia.

Location
Plaça Sant Jaume

Metro
Jaume I (L4)

Well worth seeing is the imposing inner courtyard in the Gothic style; on
the first floor is the Chapel of St George, also Gothic. At the back of the
building lies the charming orangery.
The inside of the building is open to the public on 23 April (feast day of Sant
Jordi). It is also possible to visit on Saturday or Sunday, but a written

Palau de la Generalitat, seat of the Government of Catalonia

Palau de la Generalitat

Palau de la Mùsica Catalana

Box-office . . .   *. . . and glass dome*

request must be made at least fifteen days in advance. For further information about visits, enquire at any tourist office.
To the north it adjoins the Audencia, once the court-house; the Carrer del Bisbe, leading to the Cathedral (see entry), is spanned by a charming Gothic building.

**Palau de la Música Catalana

K 4 · c 3

On the north-western edge of the old town, set back a little from the northern side of the Via Laietana, stands the Palau de la Música Catalana (Palace of Music); opened in 1908, it is one of the architect Lluis Domènech i Montaner's most unconventional modernistic designs. Although some extensions have since been added the building still retains its original appearance. The interior, with some 1700 seats, is open to the public only when concerts are held.

Location
Carrer Pau Claris

Metro
Urquinaona (L1, L4)

This large concert hall displays the full glory of the Catalan Art Nouveau style, with the flowing stucco work and beamed ceilings deserving special mention. It possesses its own chamber orchestra, and performances range from classical to contemporary and experimental music, jazz and pop.

Palau de la Virreina

J 4 · b 3

The Palau de la Virreina (Palace of the Vicereine) was built between 1772 and 1777 as a residence for Manuel d'Amat i de Junyent, then viceroy in Peru, and named after the vicereine, who continued to live here after his death until 1791. The façade displays Classical features, while the interior is Late Baroque.

Location
Rambla 99

Metro
Liceu (L3)

Nowadays the building is the headquarters of the Ajuntament's department of culture, featuring changing exhibitions and offering tickets for municipally sponsored events.

Until recently the Museu d'Arts Decoratives (see entry) and the Gabinet Postal (Postal Museum; see Palau de Pedralbes) were housed in this palace. At present the Palau de la Virreina is being renovated and the museums laid out afresh. The collections from the Gabinet Numismàtic are housed here temporarily while a permanent home is being sought.

Museums

Palau Episcopal

J 4 · c 2

The Palau Episcopal (Episcopal Palace) in the Barri Gòtic adjoins the cathedral (see entry) on the west. It was first recorded as long ago as 926; the oldest parts of the present building date from the 12th, 13th and 15th c. Renovation work was carried out in 1883 and again in 1928. The two round towers on the Portal del Bisbe date from Roman times. The inner courtyard, with its Romanesque arcades, contains a modern statue of Our Lady from the Montserrat (see entry).

Location
Plaça Nova

Metro
Liceu (L3)
Jaume I (L4)

*Palau Güell

J 3 · b 2

In 1886 the architect Antoni Gaudí was instructed by his patron, Eusebi Güell, to build an upper-class residence on a plot of land measuring only 18 × 22m/60 × 73ft, on the Carrer Nou de la Rambla, a narrow street in the old town.

Location
Carrer Nou de la
Rambla 3–5

Metro
Drassanes, Liceu
(L3)

Eusebi Güell was a great patron of the arts, and he wished to see this reflected in the palace: in the very centre of the building a large domed hall

Palau Moja

Open
Mon.–Fri. 4–8pm;
Closed Sat., Sun.
and public holidays

– intended to be used for poetry readings and private concerts – extends from the first floor right up to the roof. Around it are grouped the living rooms; the ground floor, which opens on to the street through two parabolic portals with artistic wrought-iron grilles bearing the letters E and G, Eusebi Güell's initials, housed the stables. The entire building reflects Güell's enormous wealth, with its sumptuous décor, valuable textiles and individually designed furniture, most of it by Gaudí. Here, perhaps more than in any other building, we see the ostentatious – today perhaps almost comical – imagination of the master builder. Even the roof was not forgotten when it came to art, as the dome and chimney – like those on the Casa Milà – come across as elements of decorative sculpture.

Museu de les Arts
de l'Espectacle

The Museu d'Art Escènic, from which the present Museu de les Arts de l'Espectacle (Museum of Performing Arts) has developed, was moved to the Palau Güell in 1954. It contains costumes, stage sets, models, theatrical notices and documents, some dealing with the Realistic School of Catalan dramatic art and some with ballet, etc., manuscripts and personal memorabilia relating to important actors and actresses. There are temporary exhibitions drawn from the rich fund of special material owned by the museum.

There is also a specialist library.

Palau Moja

See Eglesia de Betlem

**Palau Nacional   E 4

Location
Mirador del Palau
Nacional

Metro
Plaça d'Espanya
(L1, L3)
then Bus 61

Temporarily closed

Some distance from the Plaça d'Espanya (see entry), above the Exhibition Grounds (see entry), at the top of a wide flight of steps, stands the giant domed and architecturally somewhat over-ornate Palau Nacional (National Palace), which has been the home of the Museum of Catalan Art since 1934. The palace, originally built for the World Exhibition of 1929, is currently being completely revamped by the Italian architect Gae Aulenti. As it is not yet known when the work will be completed the Museu d'Art de Catalunya is closed to visitors until further notice; the following description relates to the pre-1992 situation. The Museu de Cèramica has finally been transferred to the Palau de Pedralbes (see entries).

**Museu d'Art de Catalunya

Temporarily closed
to visitors

The Museu d'Art de Catalunya (Museum of Catalan Art), with its splendid collections covering all periods of the history of Catalan art, is one of the most important places to visit in Barcelona.

Romanesque

The world-ranking Department of Romanesque Art (11th–13th c.) is particularly impressive. Here can be seen magnificent frescoes from many churches in the Pyrenean region of Catalonia. For this purpose, vaulted ceilings and apses from the original sites have been exactly reproduced with the wall-paintings incorporated in them, while faithful copies of the originals have replaced them in the churches from which they were taken. Photographs, ground-plans and drawings of the churches concerned accompany the exhibits. Particularly noteworthy is the room with apses from Burgal and Santa Maria d'Aneu facing each other. Also worth seeing are the frescoes from Tahull, with the nave of the local church of Santa Maria completely reproduced. Note also the liturgical articles, altar-pieces, pillar capitals and sculptured figures.

Gothic

The Department of Gothic Art (14th and 15th c.) is partly arranged systematically rather than chronologically. Its collections are not limited to Cata-

Maiestas Domini . . .

. . . and an archangel

Park . . .

. . . and Palau de Pedralbes

Palau Nacional

Cascades in the Park de la Ciutadella

Park de la Ciutadella

Park del l'Espanya Industrial

Ionia, but also include works from other regions of Spain. On display are wooden and stone sculptures, altar-pieces (including a massive 14th c. Altar to Our Lady by members of the Serra family of artists who worked in Barcelona between 1357 and 1405.

This relatively small department also contains items from other areas of Spain as well as from the Spanish Netherlands.

Renaissance
Baroque

Jardins Maragall

Opposite the main entrance to the Palau Nacional lie the impeccably maintained gardens known as the Jardins Maragall (named after the Catalan poet Joan Maragall i Gorina, 1860–1911), in which stands the Palau Albeniz, built in 1929 and with murals by Salvador Dalí. As the palazzo is now used to provide accommodation for state visitors it is not often open to the public.

Open
Sun., public
holidays
10am–2pm

Palau de Reial Pedralbes   D 9

The Palau Reial de Pedralbes lies in the similarly named and well-to-do residential area of the city, close to the Zona Universitaria in a beautiful, carefully tended and terraced park with many old cedar and lime trees. The gardens were designed by the Frenchman Jean-Claude Forestier.
At one time a country house belonging to Count Güell stood here; he subsequently made the land available for the building of a prestigious royal palace. The three-storey building in the Italian style was officially opened on the occasion of the visit of the Spanish King and Queen in 1924. The ground floor with the throne-room and large adjoining rooms is now used for public functions.
The first and second floors now permanently house the Museu de Ceràmica (see entry); the collections of the Museu d'Arts Decoratives and the Gabinet Postal (see entries) are provisionally stored here, so they are not open to the public.
The Finca Güell (see entry) adjoins the park to the north.

Location
Avinguda Diagonal
686

Metro
Palau Reial (L3)

Temporarily closed

Parc de la Ciutadella   L 3–4 · d 1–2

The Parc de la Ciutadella (Citadel Park) is a large green space covering some 30 hectares/75 acres on the north-eastern edge of the old town. It was laid out on the site of the razed citadel, which Philip V had built to suppress the rebellious population and to safeguard the harbour district. Here can be found pathways, flower-covered terraces, waterfalls and monuments. One of the park's most pleasant attractions is the "Umbracle", a structure of brick and wood with the interior filled with tropical plants. As well as museums and the zoo, some local government offices (including the Parlament de Catalunya) are situated here.

Location
Passeig Picasso/
Passeig de Pujades

Metro
Barceloneta,
Ciutadella (L4)

On the south-western edge, along the Passeig Picasso, stand the Hivernacle, a large glazed iron building dating from the turn of the century (recently restored and used for exhibitions and cultural events), and the Museu de Geologica, the Museu de Zoologica (see entries) and the Palm House.

Hivernacle

In 1988, the centenary of the 1888 World Exhibition, a statue of A. Clavé was erected in the basin of a fountain behind the Zoological Museum.

Right at the rear of the park you will come to the ostentatious Cascade, supplied by a canal and containing a number of allegorical figures and gargoyles in the form of animals. In front of it stands the Music Pavilion and

Cascade

107

a giant bronze statue of a cat on which children love to play, as well as a large one of a mammoth pointing to the nearby Zoo (see entry).

| Museum d'Art Modern | See entry |

Parc de l'Espanya Industrial   E 6

Location
Carrer del Rector Triado

Metro
Sants-Estació
(L3, L5)

The large Sants railway station is the terminus for all trains to the south. Here are situated the Expo Hotel and the dominating Torre Catalunya. The Plaça Països Catalans to the north-east has been designed in a rather unfortunate modern manner, and because of its large metal roof it has been disparagingly nicknamed the "gasolinera" ("petrol station"). However, the Parc de l'Espanya, to the south-east of the railway buildings, fits quite well into its ultra-modern surroundings.

Spaced-out seats of natural stone also serve as steps down to a small artificial lake and canal, where boats can be hired; a number of towers with flood-lighting stretch as far as the eye can see. Some very young trees are growing in the lawns, and there are courts for squash and basketball. A sports hall is being built.

**Parc Güell   L 9–10

Location
Carrer Olot

Metro
Lesseps, Vallcarca
(L3)

Open
Daily from
9am–9pm
summer;
7pm spring;
5pm autumn and
winter

In the Vallcarca district of the city, between Eixample and Tibidabo (see entries), on the side of a hill lies Parc Güell, laid out between 1900–14. It was designed by Antoni Gaudí, who also had his house here. The rather difficult climb can be avoided by taking the escalator on the right of the Avinguda de l'Hospital (to the north-west of the Lesseps metro).

Along the south-eastern wall (Carrer Olot) some brightly-coloured majolica medallions spell out the name of the park. Close by the entrance, with its beautiful iron gate, is a porter's house built in a fluid style, decorated with a tower and largely covered in coloured majolica. Close by is a small bar. This is at the bottom of a twin set of symmetrical steps leading up to a hall with columns. It is divided by a fountain, with the main emphasis on a brightly-coloured salamander-like animal in majolica.

The columned hall to which the steps lead displays elements of the Greek Doric style; the outside rows of columns lean noticeably inwards, to counteract the sideways force exerted by the vaulted roof. Between the capitals of the rather gloomy and archaic-looking columns can be seen some rich polychrome decoration made of ceramic and glazed mosaics.

On the roof of this hall a wide, flat area has been laid out, the surrounding wall of which forms a long, wavy seat. This curved wall-line results in a number of individual, semi-closed conversation seats. Here visitors can observe the original decoration of multi-coloured ceramic fragments which completely covers the seats. The terrace offers a panoramic view of the city and the sea.

In the park are a number of other features designed by Gaudí: colonnades, viaducts, grottoes, etc.

Casa Museu Gaudí (in the Parc Güell)

Open Mar.–Nov:
Sun.–Fri.
10am–2pm and
4–7pm

The house in which Antoni Gaudí lived from 1906–25 stands in the middle of the park. It has been converted into a museum containing some original drawings, items from the estate and the like.

Parc Güell, a showpiece of Modernisme ▶

Parc Joan Miró

The modernistic gatehouse . . .

. . . and colourful benches

Petanque players . . .

. . . and sculpture in the Parc de Joan Miró

Parc Joan Miró (Parc de l'Escorxador)   F 5–6

Where the abattoir (escorxador) once stood is now the Parc Joan Miró (also known as Parc de l'Escorxador).

Location
Carrer de
Tarragona

The park lies on two levels. The larger (lower) part adjoins the bullring (see Plaça de Toros, Les Arenes); it has many rows of palm trees, together with bowling-greens and football pitches.

Metro
Plaça d'Espanya
(L1, L3)
Tarragona (L3)

The higher part of the park is completely paved and has a flat, square pond in which stands the statue "Dona i Ocell" ("Woman with Bird"), covered in multi-coloured ceramic fragments, the work of Joan Miró in 1983.

"Dona i Ocell"

**Passeig de Gràcia   J 5–K 7 · c 4

The Passeig de Gràcia is undoubtedly the most elegant and striking boulevard in the Eixample (see entry). It links the Plaça de Catalunya (see entry) on the edge of the old town with the Gràcia district to the north-west adjoining the Eixample, where it continues as the much narrower Carrer Gran de Gràcia.

Situation
From Plaça de
Catalunya to Plaça
Joan Carles I

Along this broad street, flanked with rows of trees, will be found numerous banks and better quality shops; note in particular the many stately houses built in the Modernist style, which give it its characteristic stamp. The typical greenish-grey relief stones used in the pavement were designed by Antoni Gaudí.

The arms of the Catalonian capital occur frequently in the many artistic wrought iron candelabra.

The Passeig de Gràcia forms the main axis through the Quadrat d'Or (see entry), which was the upper-class residential area around the turn of the century.

See entry

Casa Milà

See entry

Casa Batlló

See entry

Museu de la
Música

Pavellò Mies van der Rohe

Mies van der Rohe Pavilion

*Pavellò Mies van der Rohe   E 4–5

Location
Avinguda del
Marquès de
Comillas

Metro
Plaça d'Espanya
(L1, L3)

Shortly before the road from Poble Espanyol (see entry) reaches the Exhibition Grounds it passes the Pavellò Mies.

Ludwig Mies van der Rohe, born in 1886 and the last director of the famous Bauhaus in Dessau (Germany), designed the German Pavilion for the World Exhibition in Barcelona in 1929, and on the centenary of his birth this replica of the original pavilion was dedicated to his memory. The building's severe lines and the aesthetic effect of the materials used (glass, steel, polished natural stone) are very effective; in the air-well stands a statue of Georg Kolbe. The chairs in the pavilion were designed as the "Barcelona" model for the World Exhibition and still retain their timeless elegance.

There is also a documentation centre which works in close co-operation with the Mies van der Rohe Archives in the Museum of Modern Art in New York.

Pedralbes (district of the city)   C 10–F 13

Location
West of the city
centre

Metro
Maria Cristina,
Palau Reial, Zona
Universitaria (L3)

Pedralbes is one of the most favoured residential areas of Barcelona; the more modern of the University (see entry) buildings are also grouped in the Zona Universitaria. The King of Spain himself resides here, in the Palau de Pedralbes (see entry). The main place to visit in this suburban district, once a village and later absorbed by Barcelona, is the Convent near the end of the Avinguda de Pedralbes.

*Monestir de Pedralbes   E 11

The Monestir de Pedralbes is a Convent of the Order of St Clare, founded in 1326 by Queen Elisenda de Montcada. In front of it lies the small park known as the Jardines Reina Elisends, with cypress trees and native shrubs. The church and convent buildings are very similar in style.
Open: Tue.–Sun. 9.30am–2pm. Closed Mon.

Railway station
(FF.CC.)
Reina Elisenda

From the park a doorway in the left-hand wall of the nave leads to the interior of the single-naved Gothic Church, lined with Chapels. The broad interior is divided into two by a wall and wrought-iron screen; only one side is open to the general public, the other being reserved for the convent community. Note the 15th c. stained-glass windows and the alabaster tomb of Queen Elisenda (d. 1364), the wife of James II.

Church

The three-storey Cloister, with its pretty Renaissance fountain, is also only partly open. In the Chapter-house stands a Flemish altar. Adjoining the Cloister is the Capella de Sant Miquel with some fine Gothic wall-paintings (1346) by Ferrer Bassa.

Cloister

The whole monastery – or at least those parts which are open to the public – serves as a museum. The exhibits are arranged so as to correspond to the living conditions of the monks. On view, in addition to furnishings, are works of art covering six centuries, some from the possessions of the convent itself and others from gifts and bequests from private sources. Of particular interest are the old apothecary, the kitchen and the sick-room, as well as the main hall of the former palace. There is also an educational service associated with the museum.

Museum

See entry

Palau de
Pedralbes

See entry

Finca Güell

Plaça de Catalunya

Pedrera

See Casa Milà

*Plaça de Catalunya   J 5 · b–c 4

Metro
Catalunya (L1, L3)

The busy Plaça de Catalunya forms the north-western end of the inner-city Ramblas (see entry) and also of the core of the old town. A number of large banks are situated around this wide and spacious square; the north-west side is dominated by the Banco Espanõl de Crédito building, while on the east side stands the massive Telefónica (Telephone Exchange) edifice.

Below the level of the square, and with entrances from several sides, lies the city's principal Metro junction; in addition, the trains covering the city routes (e.g. the Ferrocarrils de la Generalitat to Tibidabo, Pedralbes and Sant Cugat del Vallés; see entries) run from here. While the Estació de França (see Stock Exchange) is being reconstructed the trains of the national railway company RENFE also use this station. Plaça de Catalunya is also the starting point for the tourist bus "Bus 100" (see Practical Information, Public Transport).

Tip

Anyone wishing to occupy one of the many seats provided here, as in other squares in the city, should remember that a small charge will be made for the privilege.

Corte Inglés

On the northern side of the square stands the large department store known as "El Corte Inglés", well-known for its large selection of regional goods and which is certainly worth a visit (open Mon.–Sat. 10am–9pm). It has an interpreter service linked to the internal telephone system, to assist foreign customers in making their purchases. On the ninth floor is a large self-service restaurant with a terrace through the windows of which there is a fine view over the centre of the city; a pause here is recommended as a pleasant break from touring Barcelona.

Plaça del Rei

See Museu d'Història de la Ciutat

Plaça d'Espanya   F 5

Metro
Plaça d'Espanya
(L1, L3)

The circular Plaça d'Espanya, with a continuous flow of vehicles passing round it, is the main traffic junction in the west of the city. This is where the Gran Via de les Corts Catalanes (usually known as "Gran Via" for short), which cuts straight across the whole of the city, and the Avinguda de la Paral.lel, which skirts the foot of Montjuïc (see entry), intersect. In the centre of the open space stands the lavish memorial fountain "España Ofrecida a Dios" ("Spain dedicated to God").

On the southern side the entrance to the Exhibition Grounds (see entry) is formed by two towers modelled on the bell-towers of St Mark's in Venice, and on the north stands the large round Plaça de Toros (Les Arenes; see entry).

*Plaça Reial   J 3 · b 2

Location
Rambla

The Plaça Reial (not to be confused with Plaça del Rei; see Museu d'Història de la Ciutat) is connected with the Rambla dels Caputxins (see Ramblas) by

Plaça d'Espanya: gateway to the Exhibition Grounds

Plaça Reial in the Old Town

Metro
Drassanes, Liceu
(L3)

a short diagonal road (Carrer Colom). This beautiful square is enclosed by houses in the Classical style, the ground floors of which include arcades with shops and restaurants.

The square was laid out in the middle of the 19th c. on the site of a former Capuchin monastery. Among palm trees in the centre stands the beautiful Fountain of the Three Graces; the candelabra was designed by Antoni Gaudí. On Sundays the square is the busy scene of a coin and stamp market.

In recent years the square has increasingly become the haunt of drug addicts.

Plaças de Toros (Plaças de Braus)   F 5 and M 5

Location
Gran Via de les
Corts Catalanes

Barcelona possesses two bullrings (known as Plaças de Toros or Plaças de Braus). One, "Les Arenes" (Gran Via 385), adjoins the Plaça d'Espanya, while the other, "La Monumental", lies at the north-eastern end of the Gran Via (No. 747) and the Plaça de les Glóries, where Gran Via and the Diagonal cross.

"Les Arenes"

The wide, circular "Arenes", 52m/172ft in diameter, and with seats for some 15,000 spectators, was built around 1930. No bull-fights are held here nowadays. You should note the large butterfly made from multi-coloured china mosaics on the front of the "Casa de la Papallona" near the arena (architect: Josep Graner i Prat).

"Monumental"

The "Monumental" is the only ring where bullfights ("corridas") are still held. It also has a bullfighting museum.

For general information about bullfighting see Introduction, Customs and Traditions. For season and times see Practical Information, Bullfighting.

Les Arenes, bullfighting ring

Planetarium G 10

As well as the one in the Museu de la Ciència (see entry) Barcelona has another planetarium in the Carrer de les Escoles Pies. By means of complicated projection apparatus practically every conceivable phenomenom and constellation in the heavens can be portrayed. Computer technology facilitates impressive audio-visual simulations. Demonstrations (Mon.–Fri. at 9.30, 10 30 and 11.30am and 3, 4 and 5pm; Sun. and public holidays noon, 1.30 and 6.30pm; closed Sat.) are excellently supervised aand accompanied by expert commentary.

Location
Carrer de les Escoles Pies

Railway station
(FF.CC.) Sarrià

Poble Espanyol (plan see pages 118/119) D–E 4–5

In the western part of the extensive parkland on Montjuïc (see entry) is the Poble Espanyol ("Spanish Village"), laid out for the 1929 World Exhibition, it displays the building styles which are typical of the various provinces of Spain. Many well-known artists were involved in choosing, modelling and planning the lay-out.

The Poble Espanyol numbers among the most popular places to visit in Barcelona. As in most Spanish country towns, the houses are grouped around the main square, the "plaça maior", near the massive entrance gate. Near the entrance are information kiosks, the branch of a bank, book and souvenir shops. Open-air events are also held here from time to time.

Location
Avinguda Marquès de Comillas

Metro
Plaça d'Espanya, then bus 61

Open
Daily 9am–2am on Sun. and Mon., 4am Tues. and Wed., 6am Thur.–Sat. and public holidays.

West of the main square lie a number of picturesque little streets and alleyways, with glimpses of some beautiful little courtyards. A surprisingly

Poble Espanyol: the main square . . .   *. . . and a picturesque inner courtyard*

Poble Espanyol

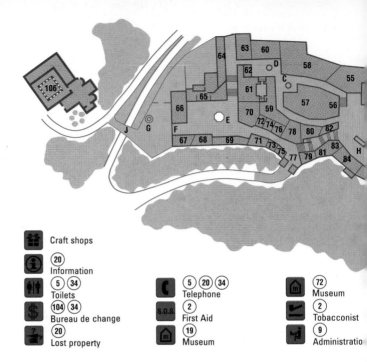

Craft shops
(20) Information
(5) (34) Toilets
(104) (34) Bureau de change
(20) Lost property

(5) (20) (34) Telephone
(2) First Aid
(19) Museum

(72) Museum
(2) Tobacconist
(9) Administratio

ORIGINAL LOCATIONS OF BUILDINGS, REPLICAS OF WHICH ARE IN THE "SPANISH VILLAGE"

1 Avila
2 Cáceres
3 Miajadas (Cáceres)
4 Plasencia
5 Cáceres
6 Sigüenza (Guadalajara)
7 Sigüenza (Guadalajara)
8 Navalcarnero (Madrid)
9 Santillana de Mar (Santander)
10 Borja (Zaragoza)
11 Riaza (Segovia)
12 Santillana del Mar (Santander)
13 Alquézar (Huesca)
14 El Burgo de Osma (Soria)
15 El Burgo de Osma (Soria)
16 Aranda de Duero (Burgos)
17 Sigüenza (Guadalajara)
18 Cambados (Pontevedra)
19 Cáceres
20 Cáceres
21 La Fresneda (Teruel)
22 La Fresneda (Teruel)
23 Sangüesa (Navarra)
24 Graus (Huesca)
25 Jérica (Castellón)

26 Montblanch (Tarragona)
27 Sigüenza (Guadalajara)
28 Segovia
29 Toledo
30 Valderrobres (Teruel)
31 Cambados (Pontevedra)
32 Cambados (Pontevedra)
33 San Esteban de Lorenzana (Lugo)
34 Medinaceli (Soria)
35 Maluenda (Zaragoza)
36 Betanzos (La Coruña)
37 Betanzos (La Coruña)
38 Caldas de Reyes (Pontevedra)
39 Cangas de Onis (Oviedo)
40 Morella (Castellón)
41 Molinos de Duero (Soria)
42 Calaceite (Teruel)
43 Catí (Castellón)
44 Jérica (Castellón)
45 Peñafiel (Valladolid)
46 Sariñena (Huesca)
47 Fraga (Huesca)
48 Borja (Zaragoza)
49 Albarracín (Teruel)
50 Albarracín (Teruel)

SPANISH VILLAGE

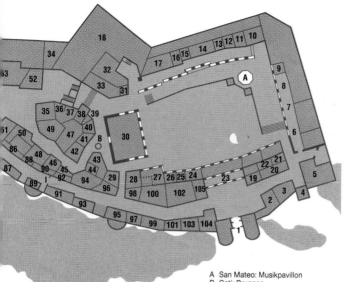

A San Mateo: Musikpavillon
B Catí: Brunnen
C Tarifa: Brunnen
D Córdoba: Virgen de los Faroles
E Prades: Brunnen
F Prades: Puerta de Prades
G Ulldecona: Wegkreuz
I Maya: Torbogen
J Ribes de Fresser

51 Corella (Navarra)
52 Alcañiz (Teruel)
53 Torralba de Ribota (Zaragoza)
54 Utebo (Zaragoza)
55 Ronda (Málaga)
56 Arcos de la Frontera (Cádiz)
57 Córdoba und Sevilla
58 Ecija (Sevilla)
59 Córdoba
60 Ubeda (Jaén)
61 Murcia
62 Córdoba
63 Arcos de la Frontera (Cádiz)
64 Mallorca
65 La Jana (Castellón)
66 Tárrega (Lérida)
67 Cornudella (Tarragona)
68 La Gárriga (Barcelona)
69 Santa Pau (Girona)
70 Besalú (Girona)
71 Rupit (Barcelona)
72 Rupit (Barcelona)
73 Isona (Lérida)
74 Montblanch (Tarragona)
75 Rupit (Barcelona)
76 Camprodón (Girona)
77 Montblanch (Tarragona)
78 Montblanch (Tarragona)

79 Besalú (Girona)
80 Rupit (Barcelona)
81 Belianes (Lérida)
82 Morella (Castellón)
83 Santa Pau (Girona)
84 Vitoria
85 Vergara (Guipúzcoa)
86 Estella (Navarra)
87 Erandio (Vizcaya)
88 Roncal (Navarra)
89 Maya (Navarra)
90 Olazagutia (Navarra)
91 Vinuesa (Soria)
92 Molinos de Duero (Soria)
93 Vinuesa (Soria)
94 Sos del Rey (Zaragoza)
95 Toro (Zamora)
96 Toro (Zamora)
97 Segovia
98 Toro (Zamora)
99 Santillana del Mar (Santander)
100 Burgo de Osma (Soria)
101 Ayllón (Segovia)
102 Ayllón (Soria)
103 Sigüenza (Guadalajara)
104 Cáceres
105 Torija (Guadalajara)
106 Monasterio (Girona)

large number of craft-workers have been established here and offer for sale some fine examples of their art; glass, ceramics, enamel-work, textiles, leather goods, prints and so on will be found in colourful abundance and at reasonable prices. Visitors are usually welcome to look around the workshops.

The village is now owned by a private company and has been extensively renovated. A new entertainment centre was added in 1988 with bars, restaurants, clubs and a theatre tent, as well as a children's theatre. A popular attraction is the "Barcelona Experience", a 22-minute audio-visual presentation of the city with commentary in English (through headphones).

Open
Tues.–Sun.
9am–2pm;
Closed Mon.

Museu d'Arts, Indústries i Tradicions Populars
Just through the entrance gate, to the right in Carrer de la Conquesta, we come to the Museu d'Arts, Indústries i Tradicions Populars (Museum of The Arts, Industry and Popular Traditions). It is a branch of the Museu Etnològic, containing its Spanish and Catalan departments.

Open
At present under
re-organisation

Museu de les Arts Gràfiques
The Poble Espanyol also incorporates the Museu de les Arts Gràfiques (Museum of Graphic Art). On display are wood and metal relief plates, old printing presses and various examples of textual and graphic printing.
Guided tours: By prior arrangement

*Port   A 1–K 3 · b–c 1

Location
In the east of the
city area

The port (Port Franc de Barcelona), with its outer harbour of about 300 hectares/740 acres , occupies the whole of the coastal strip between the district of Barceloneta (see entry) and the southern foothills of Montjuïc (see entry). Before Spain showed renewed interest in the Atlantic and her

Customs Office and Harbour, seen from the Columbus Monument

possessions in Central and South America in the 17th c., the port of Barcelona was one of the most influential in the Mediterranean, and even today
ranks as the most important in the whole of Spain. The northern end of the
harbour area and the stretch of coastline lying beyond Barceloneta are at
present being substantially reorganised and rebuilt specially for the Olympic Games.

The merchant port extends from the foot of Montjuïc, from which it is
separated by the broad Cinturó del Litoral (an arterial road leading to the
airport and on to Tarragona). With the ports of Gijón and Bilbao it is the
most modern in Spain; the annual volume of traffic is about 18 million tons.
The main imports are oil, coal, wheat and cotton; first and foremost among
its exports are wine, olive oil and cork.

For tourists, by far the most interesting part of the port is the north-eastern
section. The Moll de Barcelona, which borders it to the south, is the landing
place for passenger and ferry boats travelling to the Balearic Islands of
Mallorca, Menorca and Ibiza.

**Columbus monument

At the Plaça del Portal de la Pau stands the Monument a Cristòfor Colom
(Columbus monument), 60m/197ft high and weighing 205 tons, which was
erected for the World Exhibition in 1888. The iron column is completely
covered with allegorical figures. Around the base is a series of reliefs
depicting important stages in Columbus's life and voyages of discovery.
On the top of the column is an 8m/26ft high statue of Columbus, which
points out to sea (and therefore not directly towards the New World). A lift
takes visitors up to a look-out area from where there are excellent views of

Moll de la Fusta, a popular harbour promenade

Quadrant d'Or

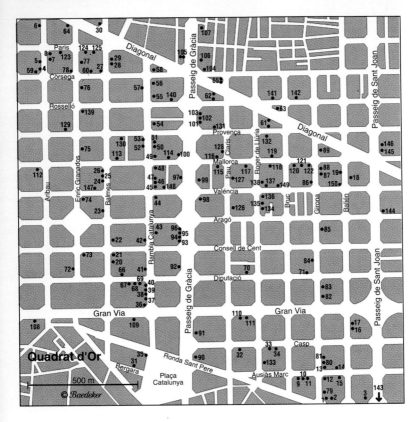

1 Casa Victorià de la Riva
   Carrer Ali Bei 1
   Enric Sagnier i Villavecchia
2 Casa Modest Andreu
   Carrer Ali Bei 3
   Telm Fernàndez i Janot
3 Cases Joaquim i Antoni Marfà
   Carrer Ali Bei 27–29
4 Casa Joaquim Cairó
   Carrer Aribau 149 bis
   Domènech Boada i Piera
5 Casa Conrad Roure
   Carrer Aribau 155
   Ferran Romeu i Ribot
6 Cases Pascual i Cia
   Carrer Aribau 175–177
   Antoni Millàs i Figuerola

7/8 Casa Societat Torres
   Germans
   Carrer Aribau 178
   Jaume Torres i Grau
9/10 Cases Manuel Felip
   Carrer Ausiàs Marc 16–20
   Telm Fernàndez i Janot
11 Casa Antonia Puget
   Carrer Ausiàs Marc 22
   Roc Cot i Cot
12 Cases Francesc Borés
   Carrer Ausiàs Marc 30–32
   Francesc Berenguer i Mestres
13 Cases Antoni Roger
   Carrer Ausiàs Marc 33–35
   Enric Sagnier
   i Villavecchia

14 Cases Tomàs Roger
   Carrer Ausiàs Marc 37–39
   Enric Sagnier
   i Villavecchia
15 Casa Antònia Borés
   Carrer Ausiàs Marc 46
   Juli Batllevell i Arús
16 Casa Francesc de Paula Vallet
   Carrer Bailén 36
   Gabriel Borell
   i Cardona
17 Casa Jaume Sahis
   Carrer Bailèn 48
   Josep Pérez i Terraza
18/19 Casa Rossend Capellades
   Carrer Bailén 126
   Jeroni Granell i Manresa

20/21 Cases Josep J. Bertrand
   Carrer Balmes 44–50
   Enric Sagnier i Villavecchia
22 Cases Antoni Miquel
   Carrer Balmes 54
   Jeroni Granell i Manresa
23 Casa Jeroni Granell
   Carrer Balmes 65
   Jeroni Granell i Manresa
24 Cases Joan Pons
   Carrer Balmes 81
   Joan Pons i Trabal
25 Casa Jaume Larcegui
   Carrer Balmes 83
   Eduard Mercader i Sacanell
26 Cases Frederic Vallet Xiró
   Carrer Balmes 85–87
   Josep Maria Barenys
   i Gambús
27 Casa Josep Filella
   Carrer Balmes 149
   Manuel J. Raspall i Mayol
28 Casa Francesc Fargas
   Carrer Balmes 156
   Francesc Fargas i Margenat
29 Cases Adolf Ruiz
   Carrer Balmes 158–160
   Adolf Ruiz i Casamitjana
30 Casa Lluís Pérez Samanillo
   Carrer Balmes 166–169
   Joan Hervas i Arzimendi
31 Casa Emilia Carles de Tolrà
   Carrer Bergara 11
   Emili Sala i Cortès
32 Casa Llorenç Camprubí
   Carrer Casp 22
   Adolf Ruiz i Casamitjana
33 Casa Antoni Salvadó
   Carrer Casp 46
   Juli Batllevell i Arús
34 Casa Calvet
   Carrer Casp 48
   Antoni Gaudí
35 Casa Bosch i Alsina
   Plaça de Catalunya 8
   Joaquim Bassegoda i Amigó und
   Pere Bassegoda i Mateu
36 Casa Pia Batlló
   Rambla de Catalunya 17
   Josep Vilaseca
   i Casanovas
37 Casa Heribert Pons
   Rambla de Catalunya 19–21
   Alexandre Soler i March
38 Casa Jaume Moysi
   Rambla de Catalunya 23
   Manuel Comas i Thos
39 Casa Sebastià Pratjusà
   Rambla de Catalunya 25
   Antoni Serra i Pujals
40 Casa Climent Asols
   Rambla de Catalunya 27
   Francesc del Villar i Carmona
41 Casa Rodolf Juncadella
   Rambla de Catalunya 33
   Enric Sagnier i Villavecchia
42 Casa Miquel A. Fargas
   Rambla de Catalunya 47
   Enric Sagnier i Villavecchia
43 Casa Dolors Calm
   Rambla de Catalunya 54
   Josep Vilaseca i Casanovas

44 Casa Bonaventura Pollés
   Rambla de Catalunya 72
   Bonaventura Pollés i Vivó
45 Casa Asunción Belloso
   de Gabriel
   Rambla de Catalunya 74
   Josep Domènech i Estapà
46/47 Casa Evarist Juncosa
   Rambla de Catalunya 76
   Salvador Viñals i Sabaté
48 Casa Francesc Farreras
   Rambla de Catalunya 86
   Josep Pérez i Terraza
49 Casa Josep i Ramón Queraltó
   Rambla de Catalunya 88
   Josep Plantada i Artigas
50 Casa Pilar i Josefa Albiñana de
   Regàs
   Rambla de Catalunya 92–94
   Francesc Berenguer
   i Mestres
51 Casa Ferran Cortés
   Rambla de Catalunya 96
   Enric Sagnier i Villavecchia
52/53 Casa Manuel Verdú
   Rambla de Catalunya 101/103
   Maurici Augé
55 Cases Godó-Lallana
   Rambla de Catalunya 112
   Josep Majó i Ribas
56 Casa Antònia Costa
   Rambla de Catalunya 122
   Josep Domènech i Estapà
57 Casa Llorenç Armengol
   Rambla de Catalunya 125
   Adolf Ruiz i Casamitjana
58 Casa Serra
   Rambla de Catalunya 126
   Josep Puig i Cadafalch
59 Casa Antoni Piera
   Carrer Còrsega 239
   Domènech Boada i Piera
60 Casa Pau Martí
   Carrer Còrsega 271
   Domènech Boada i Piera
61 Casa Pilar Bassols
   Diagonal 355
   Gabriel Borrell i Cardona
62 Palau Baró de Quadras
   Josep Puig i Cadafalch
63 Casa Terrades (Casa de les
   Punxes)
   Diagonal 416/420
   Josep Puig i Cadafalch
64 Casa Miquel Sayrach
   Diagonal 423/425
   Manuel Sayrach i Carreras
65 Casa Comalat
   Diagonal 442
   Salvador Valeri i Pupurull
66 Casa Josep J. Bertrand
   Carrer Diputació 235/237
   Enric Sagnier i Villavecchia
67 Casa Clapés
   Carrer Diputació 246
   Joaquim Bassegoda i Amigó
68 Casa Miquel Ibarz
   arrer Diputació 248
   Salvador Soteres i Taberner
69 Casa Rupert Garriga Nogués
   Carrer Diputació 250
   Enric Sagnier i Villavecchia

70 Casa Marcel·li Costa
   Carrer Diputació 299
   Architekt unbekannt
71 Casa Josep Fabra
   Carrer Diputació 329
   Enric Sagnier i Villavecchia
72 Casa Antoni Pàmies
   Carrer Enric Granados 5
   Melcior Viñals i Muñoz
73 Casa Domènech i Estapà
   Carrer Enric Granados 6
   Josep Doménech i Estapà
74 Casa Leandre Bou
   Carrer Enric Granados 20
   Antoni Serrallach
75 Casa Anna Salvadó de Guitart
   Carrer Enric Granados 48
   Josep Coll i Vilaclara
76 Casa Adolf Ruiz
   Carrer Enric Granados 94
   Adolf Ruiz i Casamitjana
77 Casa Francesc Cairó
   Carrer Enric Granados 106
   Domènech Boada i Piera
78 Casa Enric Llorens
   Carrer Enric Granados 119
   Josep Pérez i Terraza
79 Casa Enric i Voctòria de la Riva
   Carrer Girona 4
   Enric Sagnier i Villavecchia
80 Casa Antoni Roger
   Carrer Girona 22
   Enric Sagnier i Villavecchia
81 Casa Enric Roger
   Carrer Girona 24
   Enric Sagnier i Villavecchia
82 Casa Ramon Vilà
   Carrer Girona 46
   Joan Maymó i Cabanellas
83 Casa Jacinta Ruiz
   Carrer Girona 54
   Ramon Viñolas i Llossas
84 Casa Esperança Isern
   Carrer Girona 67
   Roc Cot i Cot
85 Casa Isabel Pomar
   Carrer Girona 86
   Joan Rubió i Bellver
86 Casa Eduardo de Lamadrid
   Carrer Girona 113
   Lluís Domènech i Montaner
87 Casa Adolf Ruiz
   Carrer Girona 120
   Adolf Ruiz i Casamitjana
88 Casa Jeroni Granell
   Carrer Girona 122
   Jeroni F. Granell i Manresa
89 Casa Francesc Cairó
   Carrer Girona 132
   Domènec Boada i Piera
90 Cases Pons i Pasqual
   Passeig de Gràcia 2/4
   Enric Sagnier i Villavecchia
91 Cases Antoni Rocamora
   Passeig de Gràcia 6–14
   Joaquim Bassegoda i Amigó
92 Casa Manuel Margarida
   Passeig de Gràcia 27
   Joaquim Codina i Matalí
93 Casa Lleó Morera
   Passeig de Gràcia 35
   Lluís Domènech i Montaner

Quadrant d'Or – *continued*

94 Casa Ramon Mulleras
   Passeig de Gràcia 37
   Enric Sagnier i Villavecchia
95 Casa Amatller
   Passeig de Gràcia 41
   Josep Puig
   i Cadafalch
96 Casa Batlló
   Passeig de Gràcia 43
   Antoni Gaudí
97 Cases Alexandre i Josefina
   Jofre
   Passeig de Gràcia 65
   Bonaventura Bassegoda
   i Amigó
98 Casa Marfà
   Passeig de Gràcia 66
   Manuel Comas i Thos
99 Casa Joan Coma
   Passeig de Gràcia 74
   Enric Sagnier
   i Villavecchia
100 Casa Enric Batlló
   Passeig de Gràcia 75
   Josep Vilaseca i Casanovas
101 Casa Milà (La Pedrera)
   Passeig de Gràcia 92
   Antoni Gaudí
102 Casa Josep Codina
   Passeig de Gràcia 94
   Antoni Rovira i Rabassa
103 Casa Ramon Casas
   Passeig de Gràcia 96
   Antoni Rovira i Rabassa
104 Casa Rupert Garriga
   Passeig de Gràcia 112
   Enric Sagnier
   i Villavecchia
105 Casa Bonaventura Ferrer
   Passeig de Gràcia 113
   Pere Falques i Urpí
106 Casa Lluís Ferrer-Vidal
   Passeig de Gràcia 114
   Eduard Ferrés i Puig
107 Casa Fuster
   Passeig de Gràcia 132
   Lluís Domènech
   i Montaner
108 Casa Jeroni Granell
   Gran Via 582
   Jeroni F. Granell i Manresa
109 Casa Josep Portabella
   Gran Via 616
   Domènec Balet i Nadal
110 Casa Camil Mulleras Garrós
   Gran Via 654
   Enric Sagnier i Villavecchia
111 Casa Ramon Oller
   Gran Via 658
   Pau Salvat i Espasa

112 Cases Jeroni Granell
   Carrer Mallorca 184–188
   Jeroni F. Granell
   i Manresa
113 Casa Gustau Peyra
   Carrer Mallorca 235
   Enric Sagnier
   i Villavecchia
114 Casa Angel Batlló
   Carrer Mallorca 253–257
   Josep Vilaseca
   i Casanovas
115 Casa Marqués de Julià
   Carrer Mallorca 264
   Enric Sagnier
   i Villavecchia
116 Cases Amadeu Maristany
   Carrer Mallorca 273/275
   Bonaventura Bassegoda
   i Amigó
117 Palau Ramon de Montaner
   Carrer Mallorca 278
   Lluís Domènech
   i Montaner
118 Casa Francesc Farreras
   Carrer Mallorca 284
   Antoni Millàs i Figuerola
119 Casa Thomas
   Carrer Mallorca 291/293
   Lluís Domènech i Montaner
120/121 Cases Dolors Xiró de Vallet
   Carrer Mallorca 302/304
   Josep Barenys i Gambús
122 Casa Carme Carsi de Puig
   Carrer Mallorca 306
   Josep Barenys i Gambús
123 Casa Societat Torres Germans
   Carrer París 182
   Jaume Torres i Grau
124 Casa Josep Batlles
   Carrer París 202
   Francesc Ferriol i Carreras
125 Casa Teresa Vallhonrat
   Carrer París 204
   Francesc Ferriol i Carreras
126 Casa Rafael Barba
   Carrer Pau Claris 140/142
   Enric Sagnier i Villavecchia
127 Cases Leandre Bou
   Carrer Pau Claris 154/156
   Antoni Millàs i Figuerola
128 Casa Dolors Xiró de Vallet
   Carrer Pau Claris 161
   Josep Barenys i Gambús
129 Casa Segarra
   Carrer Provença 185
   Josep Masdeu i Puigdemasa
130 Casa Francesc Pastor
   Carrer Provença 258
   Enric Sagnier i Villavecchia

131 Casa Josep Ferrer-Vidal
   Carrer Provença 267/269
   Enric Sagnier i Villavecchia
132 Casa Francesc Lalanne
   Carrer Provença 324/326
   Arnau Calvet i Peyronill
133 Cases Joaquim Cabot
   Carrer Roger de Llúria 8–14
   Josep Vilaseca i Casanovas
134 Casa Pere Salisachs
   Carrer Roger de Llúria 72
   Salvador Viñals i Sabaté
135 Casa Agustí Anglora
   Carrer Roger de Llúria 74
   Isidre Raventós i Amiguet
136 Cases Castillo Villanueva
   Carrer Roger de Llúria 80
   Juli Fossas i Martínez
137 Casa Jaume Forn
   Carrer Roger de Llúria 82
   Jeroni F. Granell i Manresa
138 Casa Jeroni Granell
   Carrer Roger de Llúria 84
   Jeroni F. Granell i Manresa
139 Casa Esteve Recolons
   Carrer Rosselló 192
   Pere Bassegoda i Mateu
140 Casa Baldomer Rovira
   Carrer Rosselló 247
   Andreu Audet i Puig
141 Casa Leonor Matas
   Carrer Rosselló 293
   Jeroni F. Granell i Manresa
142 Casa Alexandre Gioan
   Carrer Rosselló 301
   Ramon Ribera i Rodriguez
143 Casa Enric Laplana
   Passeig de Sant Joan 6
   Bernardi Martotell i Puig
144 Casa Eulàlia Artés de Mayolas
   Passeig de Sant Joan 84 bis
   Salvador Viñals i Sabaté
145 Casa Macaya
   Passeig de Sant Joan 108
   Josep Puig i Cadafalch
146 Casa Dolors Alesan de Gibert
   Passeig de Sant Joan 110
   Enric Fatjó i Torras
147 Casa Martí Llorens
   Carrer València 213
   Antoni Alabern i Pomar
148 Casa Domènech i Estapà
   Carrer València 241
   Josep Domènech i Estapà
149 Casa Pau Ubarri
   Carrer València 293
   Miquel Madorell i Rius
150 Casa Manuel Llopis
   Carrer València 339
   Antoni Galissà i Soqué

Port – continued   the port and the city. On the windows transparent pictures and captions serve to facilitate the visitor's orientation.
At the foot of the monument, in the Portal de la Pau, horse-drawn carriages offer tours of the area.

South of the monument stands the imposing and rather ornate customs building (Duana).

Anchored here until a short time ago was a replica of the "Santa Maria", Columbus's flagship on his first expedition to America. It was recently destroyed, apparently by arsonists.

Open Late June–late Sept: daily 9am–9pm; late Sept.–late June: Tues.–Sat. 10am–2pm and 3.30–6.30pm; Sun. and public holidays 10am–7pm. Closed Mon.

Moll de la Fusta

The Moll de la Fusta is the name given to the section of the port between Portal de la Pau and the Plaça d'Antoni Lòpez. The Moll de Bosch i Alsina, which runs directly parallel, is linked to it by two railway bridges and has been turned into a spacious promenade with seats, restaurants and an underground car-park.

On the Moll de la Fusta lies the large, extravagantly built galleon "Neptune" (viewing times: daily, 10am–8pm).

Along the harbour mole the Golondrinas ("swallows") landing-stage can be reached, from where boat-trips round the port may be taken (July–Sept: daily 10.30am–9pm; Oct.–June: Mon.–Sat. 11am–6pm, Sun. and public holidays 11am–7pm; duration approximately 30 mins). | Golondrinas

**Harbour cable car

Spanning the harbour basin diagonally is the harbour cable car (in Catalan "Transbordador Aerí"; Operating times – summer: daily 11am–9pm; winter: Mon.–Fri. noon–5.45pm, Sat., Sun. and public holidays 11.30am–7pm). The harbour terminus is the Torre de Sant Sebastian on the new mole, a 96m/315ft steel lattice mast (the Plaça del Mar with sports and cultural facilities is planned); the intermediate station is the 158m/519ft Torre de Jaume I on the Moll de Barcelona. The funicular ends on the north-east side of Montjuïc (see entry), near the Jardins Mossen Costa i Llobera (cactus garden). During the journey passengers can enjoy a splendid view of the port area and the wide Passeig de Colom.

See Museu Marítim. | Marine Museum

Expansion plans in the port area

The Moll de Barcelona (see above) is to be the site of the International Trade Centre, which on completion will have a height of 40m/131ft and a usable surface area of 80,000 sq.m/95,000 sq yds. In addition the building of a harbour promenade is planned. | Moll de Barcelona

On a platform 4.5m/14¾ft high over the wharf, a centre for leisure, culture, sports and shopping is being created, in which there will be a large cinema, an amphitheatre, restaurants as well as an aquarium, a marine museum and an underground car park. | Moll d'Espanya

A promenade and sports marina for the Olympic Games (see Olympic Sites) is being created. | Barceloneta Pier

125

**Quadrat d'Or

J–K 5–6

Location
Between the Old
Town and the
Diagonal

Metro
Catalunya (L1, L3),
Passeig de Gràcia
(L3, L4),
Diagonal (L3, L5)

See plan pp.
122–124

Casa Calvet

"Quadrat d'Or" ("Golden Quarter") is the name given to that area of the Eixample (see entry) containing the best and most numerous examples of the Modernist style of architecture. It is bordered mainly by the Plaça de Catalunya to the south, by the Avinguda de la Diagonal to the north, by the Passeig de Sant Joan to the north and Carrer Muntaner to the south-west. The main road through it is the Passeig de Gràcia (see entry).

What gives the Quadrat d'Or its special charm is the large number of well-preserved late 19th and early 20th c. residences designed by a number of different architects and thus providing a varied cross-section of the Modernist style. Literally at every step the visitor will stumble across interesting details – ceramic art, stained glass windows, wrought-iron work, reliefs, mosaics, statues and much more besides – a genuine "open-air" museum.

The Ramblas . . .

. . . with street-theatre

**Ramblas

J 3–7 · b 1–4

The Rambles (here better known under their Catalan name of "Ramblas"), the principal thoroughfare in the city centre, stretches north-westward from the Columbus Memorial near the Port (see entry). The 1180m/1290yds long section to the Plaça de Catalunya (see entry) is lined with plane trees; with its wide pedestrian zone flanked by a narrow road on each side it is a favourite place for a stroll, and is one of Barcelona's main attractions. To the right (north-east) lies the Barri Gòtic, to the left (south-west) the Barri Xino (see entries). As well as its flower and bird market the Ramblas boasts a considerable number of book and newspaper stands, restaurants and cafés with tables in the open. The pavement artists, street musicians and other impromptu performers all add to its distinctive atmosphere; but be warned against getting involved in any games of chance! It is also unfortunately true to say that pickpockets and tricksters find rich pickings here.

Location
between Barri Gòtic and Barri Xino

Metro
Catalunya (L1; also FF.CC.), Drassanes, Liceu, Catalunya (L3)

Rambla de Santa Monica

Near the Columbus Memorial (see Port) is the start of the Rambla de Santa Monica. Right at the beginning of the street, on the left, lies the Naval Command Headquarters; a few steps further, at the corner of the Portal de Santa Madrona, is the Centre d'Art Santa Monica, with some high quality temporary art exhibitions, and the parish church of the same name. The Waxworks (see Museu de Cera) lies on the other side of the Rambla.

Rambla dels Caputxins

From the Rambla dels Caputxins the Carrer Nou de la Rambla branches off on the left; here stands the Palau Güell (see entry). An opening on the right leads to the Plaça Reial (see entry). A few steps further, on the same side of the street, is the Carrer Ferran Jaume I, the shortest route to the Barri Gòtic. Further left stands the Gran Teatre del Liceu (see entry). The Rambla dels Caputxins ends at the Plaça de la Boqueria; from here the Carrer del Cardenal Casanyas leads northwards to the church of Santa Maria del Pi (see entry).

Rambla dels Flors (Rambla de Sant Josep)

On its north-western side the Plaça del Boqueria adjoins the Rambla de Sant Josep. This is where the colourful flower market is held each morning, and which has given it its popular name of the "Rambla dels Flors". On the left side are the market hall (see Mercat de Sant Josep), and the Palau de Virreina (see entry). At the junction of the Rambla and the Carrer del Carme looms the sombre and heavy façade of the Eglesia de Betlem (see entry), once the Jesuit church.

Rambla dels Estudis/Rambla Canaletes

At the junction with the Carrer del Carme is the beginning of the Rambla dels Estudis, where the bird and fish market is held in the mornings. Together with the Rambla Canaletes it forms the link with the Plaça de Catalunya (see entry).

Rambla de Catalunya

The north-western extension of the Ramblas forms the far side of the square known as the Rambla de Catalunya, which stretches from the

Towers of the Sagrada Família, bishop's mitres in stone

Eixample (see entry) to the Avinguda de la Diagonal. It has none of the flair and atmosphere of the old Ramblas, being on a par with all the other purely functional routes through the new part of the city.

*Sagrada Família M 6

The Sagrada Família church (its official name being "Temple Expiatori de la Sagrada Família", the Holy Family Church of the Atonement), is the most famous sight in Barcelona and also one of Europe's most unconventional churches. Dominating its surroundings, it stands in the northern part of the city.

Location
Plaça Gaudí

Metro
Sagrada Família
(L5)

When Antoni Gaudí was put in charge of constructing the church in 1883 plans had already been drawn up and some work done on building the crypt of what was to be a purely Neo-Gothic church. Gaudí decided to change the plans completely but – as in the case of most of his other works – had no firm ideas in mind, preferring to alter and add to the plans as work progressed. Of course, this meant that there was no question of getting it built quickly, although Gaudí had originally forecast between ten and fifteen years; there were also financial limitations, as the cost was to be met solely from alms and public subscription. As a result the "Church of the Poor", the main work by the most important Catalan architect of modern times, remains just a shell, and nobody knows whether and when it will ever be completed.

Open
Daily 9am–9pm
July and Aug., 8pm
Apr.–June and
Sept.–Dec., 7pm
Jan.–Mar.

The church is planned to have a total length of 110m/354ft and a height of 45m/148ft, with a principal dome of 160m/525ft and towers up to

◀ *Temple de la Sagrada Família*

Temple de la Sagrada Familia

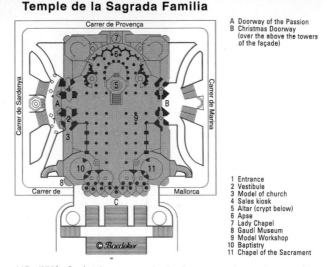

A Doorway of the Passion
B Christmas Doorway
(over the above the towers of the façade)

1 Entrance
2 Vestibule
3 Model of church
4 Sales kiosk
5 Altar (crypt below)
6 Apse
7 Lady Chapel
8 Gaudí Museum
9 Model Workshop
10 Baptistry
11 Chapel of the Sacrament

115m/378ft. So far, however, only the four-towered east doorway (the "Nativity Front"), the outer walls of the apse, the crypt in which Antoni Gaudí was buried in 1926 (not open to the public), parts of the west doorway (the "Passion Doorway") and the nave walls have been built.

From an artistic point of view the Templo de la Sagrada Família is an extremely unconventional mixture of established styles and new ideas. The ground-plan, the way the area is divided up and the firm lines strongly reflect Gothic and mid-19th c. Neo-Gothic, but are combined with the flowing, herbaceous ornamentation so typical of the Art Nouveau style.

Museum

Recently work on the main crypt which houses the museum has restarted, and it is expected that the range of exhibits will also change.
The present entrance is in the left side-crypt near the entrance, where postcards are sold. Of interest are the sketches and photographs illustrating Gaudí buildings and of the ancient ones on which they are modelled. In separate departments can be seen plaster mock-ups of the sculptured decoration; there is also a large, partially restored model of the church which was shown in Paris in 1910. The studies covering the window and façade designs clearly illustrate the principle of "diagonal supports" which Gaudí wished to see replace the Gothic buttress. Also of interest is a wire model illustrating structural engineering principles; Gaudí hung weights on an inverted wire framework to represent the anticipated stresses and strains, thus showing clearly the static base structure. To understand it fully you have to imagine the picture turned through 180 degrees.

At the end of the crypt is a large photographic reproduction of the Passion Façade; to its right is the iconography, in the Catalan dialect, of the individual motifs. There is also a multi-vision show, and in one of the side rooms a model cut in half to show the nave and side aisles.

Church

The first doorway, the west or Passion Doorway, has been added to in recent years. There is a striking difference in styles between the sculpture forms (by José Maria Subirach) used here and the other decoration influenced by Gaudí. Note the portrayal of Christ wearing a veil; it is in bas-relief

Interior of the apse . . .   . . . and view from the east tower

and produces the optical illusion that the head is moving closer to the observer.

Through the entrance stands the large plaster model of the church (scale 1:25), showing the Passion Façade; here too are a number of water-colours of the other fronts and doorways.

The broad interior is still a building site with several rotary cranes; pre-fabricated building sections give a close-up idea of the form it will take. Where the transepts and apse meet stands the altar protected by a canopy, under which lies the main crypt (where Antoni Gaudí was interred in 1926; normally closed).

The towers of the right side doorway (Nativity Doorway) can be climbed, but the open, narrow winding staircase makes it a rather unattractive proposition for anybody prone to giddiness. Nearby is an ancient lift; it is worthwhile going up in this to enjoy the fantastic view over the city and of the helm roofs of the towers, clad in colourful majolica, reminiscent of bishops' mitres.

**View

The small building nearby with the undulating roof, once the builders' hut, is now used as offices and is not open to the public.

Santa Anna

J 4 · c 3

In a narrow street a little to the east of the Plaça de Catalunya (see entry) stands the Convent of Santa Anna, founded in the 12th c. by the Order of the Holy Sepulchre and dissolved in 1835. The cloister and chapter-house, both of which still remain, were built in the 15th c.; many other parts from the same period were pulled down in the 19th c.

Location
Carrer Rivadeneyra

Metro
Catalunya (L1, L3)

Santa Maria del Mar

Passage near Santa Maria del Pí

Originally Romanesque in style, the church has a cruciform ground plan and rectangular choir. The interior has round arches and was partially altered in the 14th c.; its small Romanesque windows provide little light. The tabernacle is a copy of the 15th/16th c. original, which has long since disappeared.

The 14th c. Chapel of the Blessed Sacrament lies to the left of the entrance. In it will be found some modern paintings and a 15th c. burial group.

From the church there is access to the cloister and thence to the chapter-house.

*Santa Maria del Mar   K 3 · c–d 2

Location
Plaça Montcada

Metro
Jaume I (L4)

Open
Daily 8am–1pm and
5–8pm

On the Carrer Montcada, a little way south of the Museu Picasso (see entry), stands the church of Santa Maria del Mar (1329–83), a triple-aisled Gothic edifice with no transept. After the Cathedral (see entry) it is the most important ecclesiastical building in the city. It occupies the site of a Late Roman necropolis where, according to legend, St Eulalia was buried.

A large rose-window opens above the richly decorated main door; the sumptuous interior gives an harmonious impression of space. Most of the stained glass dates from the 15th–17th c.; in the chapel near the left side door can be seen a black Madonna. Note also the stone bosses in the vaulting; the Coronation of Our Lady is depicted above the main altar. On the main altar stands a Gothic statue of the Madonna, and in front of it a model of an old trading ship. Below the raised chancel is the entrance to the crypt. The church is currently undergoing restoration work, so access cannot be guaranteed.

The small square on the right of the church is taken up by a memorial, sunken after the manner of an amphitheatre. On the long walls of polished natural stone is a dedication to the Catalans who died in battle against the troops of Philip V in 1714.

Memorial

*Santa Maria del Pí   J 4 · b 2

On the little Plaça del Pí in the old town stands the Gothic church of Santa Maria del Pí (Our Blessed Lady of the Pine Tree). The otherwise rather sober main façade is relieved by a pointed-arch doorway with a Gothic statue of the Madonna and by a large rose-window. The main tower and those on the front have no domes.

Location
Plaça del Pí

Metro
Liceu (L3)

The single-aisled, plain interior is flanked by chapels; the clerestory possesses stained glass windows from the 15th–18th c., those in the rose window being copies of the originals which were destroyed in 1936. Near the door to the sacristy lies the Gothic tomb of Arnau Ferre, who died in 1394 at the siege of Catania in Sicily.
The treasury contains gold and silversmith work and other sacred art.

The left-hand wall of the nave adjoins the pretty, shady Plaça de Sant Josep Oriol, with some attractive shop entrances. Under the trees in the middle of the square stands a memorial to the poet and dramatist Angel Guimerá i Jorge (1845–1924).

Plaça de Sant
Josep Oriol

The little Plaça del Pí (see above) leads to a glass-roofed shopping precinct with several streets crossing it; in the Barri del Pi, where it widens out, are a surprisingly large number of art, antique and jewellery shops.

Barri del Pí

Sant Cugat del Vallès   outside the area of the city plan

The little town of Sant Cugat del Vallès, lies some 15km/9½ miles northwest of Barcelona. The best road goes via Valvidrera; more scenic, but narrower and winding, is the alternative road via the Tibidabo (see entry). A rail connection from the Plaça de Catalunya (see entry) can be made with the trains of the Ferrocarrils de la Generalitat (FF.CC.).

Location
15km/9½ miles to
the north-west

Railway station
(FF.CC.)
Sant Cugat

Benedictine monastery

The first documented record of the former Benedictine monastery was in 897; the present Romanesque-Gothic edifice dates from the 12th–17th c. and is therefore not unified in style. The cloister area, so steeped in atmosphere, is still largely walled.

Open
Mon., Wed., Fri.
10am–12 noon
(church):
Tues.–Sat.
10am–2pm and
4pm–7pm (cloister)

The main front of the triple-aisled church is relatively low and stocky with a plain Gothic doorway, dominated by a large rose-window above and two smaller ones at the side. The choir section, with a main apse and two side apses, is Romanesque, but with a plain tracery window in the former. Also Gothic are the stump of the crossing-tower and the windows in the side-aisles. Inside can be seen a beautiful Altar to the Blessed Sacrament (1375) and the tomb of Abbot Odo (14th c.).

On the left of the church front is the entrance to the cloister. Note in particular the 150 or so capitals decorated with figures.

Sant Pau del Camp   H 3 · a 2

The church of Sant Pau del Camp (St Paul-in-the-Field) owes its name to the fact that it was built outside the town boundary at the time, i.e. actually in a

Location
Carrer Sant Pau

Metro
Paral.lel (L3)

field. The Avinguda de la Paral.lel now runs through here, forming the boundary between the old town (see Barri Xino) and the new development at the foot of Montjuïc (see entry).

Sant Pau del Camp is a Romanesque building dating from 1117, on a cruciform ground-plan with a triple-domed choir and a massive crossing-tower. Note the beautiful main door, with its marble capital from the West Gothic period. The groin-vaulted interior adjoins the Gothic chapter-house on its right, which in turn leads out into the cloister.

Stock Exchange   K 3 · c–d 1

Location
Pla del Palau

Metro
Barceloneta (L4)

The Stock Exchange (Catalan: Llotja) was founded in the 14th c. when the city was at its economic zenith. Nothing has remained of the first building, which was erected close to the shore. The present-day Stock Exchange was built between 1380 and 1392 in the Late Gothic style, but was then extended and altered in the 15th, 16th and 18th c., the last such additions being in Classical forms which characterise the present-day exterior of the building. Until a few years ago the Academy of Art (Escola de Belles Arts) was also situated here.

*Gothic Room

The only part of the Stock Exchange which has not been changed since its inception is the elegant Gothic Room, a three-aisled room divided by arches resting on slender columns, in which even today the business of the Stock Exchange is still conducted.

Also of note are the staircase with its allegories of industry and trade and the purely Classical rooms of the Junta de Comerç (chamber of trade) on the upper floor.

Pla del Palau

The square adjoining the Stock Exchange to the north (Pla del Palau) is the focal point of Barcelona's maritime trade. Around it are grouped numerous offices and commercial and administrative buildings, including the Govern Civil (civil administration).

Estació de França

Further to the north and to the right is the Estació de França, the station for France, with rail connections to the north. At present it is being enlarged, together with the adjoining area, to provide a national and international terminal. Meanwhile the Plaça de Catalunya (see entry) has taken over the function of the station.

Temple de la Sagrada Família

See Sagrada Família

**Tibidabo   H–J 13

Location
north-west of the
town centre

Railway station
Avinguda del
Tibidabo,
then by bus or
Tramvia
Blau (Blue Tram)
and cableway

To the north-west of the city centre rises Tibidabo, 532m/1746ft high and one of the most popular tourist destinations in the Barcelona district. It derives its name from the legend which says that it was here that Christ was tempted by the devil with the words "I will give you . . .", the Latin for which is "tibi dabo . . .".

From the Plaça de Catalunya visitors can travel by the underground railway (Ferrocarrils de la Generalitat) as far as the Avinguda del Tibidabo terminus. From here there is a nostalgic trip by tram, known as the "Tramvia Blau" because of its blue-painted coaches (note: these may be temporarily

Church of the Sagrat Cor . . .

. . . and view over the city

In the Parc d'Atraccions on Tibidabo

Tibidabo
Parc d'Atraccions

A–H Refreshments
I   Toilets, Telephone
L   Souvenirs

1 Pan-o-ramic
2 Atalaya
3 Roundabout
4 Rodeo
5 Tibi-Air
6 Tibi-Bobs
7 Mini-Congo

8 Montaña Rusa
9 Pasaje del Terror
10 Miralls Màgics
11 Museo Autómatas
12 Treping
13 Galaxy
14 Crash-Cars

15 Piratta
16 Viking
17 Tchu-Tchu-Tren
18 Zoochok
19 Tralla
20 Aladino
21 Diavolo

22 Alaska
23 Tibidabo Express
24 Barka Choke
25 Castillo
   Misterloso
26 Funicular

replaced by public buses), up the hill as far as the funicular cableway station for the final lap to the top. The lower station of the cableway is 223·5m/733ft above sea level, with a restaurant and a model of the Tibidabo. A road, 8km/5 miles long, also winds its way from the city up the hill.

Sagrat Cor

On the top of Tibidabo stands Sagrat Cor church (Church of the Sacred Heart), built on various levels as recently as 1961 in Gothic style by the architect Enric Sagnier. The ground floor is a building strongly reminiscent of the period around the turn of the century; in the apse a mosaic portrays people dressed in clothes worn by middle-class citizens of the time.

On the second level stands the basilica, Neo-Gothic in style and almost circular in plan; its enormous height gives the impression of great spaciousness.

A lift goes up to a platform 541.8m/1778ft above sea level, with several towers.

Steps lead to the ambulatory round the foot of the giant statue of Christ, which can be seen from miles away. From here there is a superb view of Barcelona and the sea, over the chain of mountains which includes Tibidabo and the wooded hills of the interior. To the south stands a TV mast for transmitting the Olympic Games, and to the north the transmitters of Radio Barcelona and Catalunya Radio.

**View

*Parc d'Atraccions

Most visitors to Tibidabo head for the Parc de Atraccions, an amusement park constructed on several levels on the steep mountain-side, similar to that on the Montjuïc (see entry). Dating from 1901 the amusement park has recently been renovated. There are various types of rides (roller coaster, big wheel, dodgems, go-carts) and other amusements, games of skill, computer games, several restaurants and so on. Families with children will find a visit to the park particularly worthwhile; it is best to plan to spend at least half a day there or, better still, a full day, when the visit can be combined with a visit to the Museu de la Ciència (see entry) near the lower station of the Tramvia Blau.

Open
May–Sept: daily;
Oct.–Apr: Sat., Sun.
and public
holidays;
Christmas and
Easter
holidays: daily.

As well as the normal entry ticket – which is comparatively cheap but only includes six determined attractions – there is an "all-in" ticket, which includes the use of all the facilities at no extra cost. The hours of opening vary but can be obtained from any tourist office.

Tucked in among the other attractions in the amusement park is the Museu d'Autòmats, a collection of old gaming machines, juke-boxes, mechanical dolls, model railways, etc.

Museu
d'Autòmats

Triumphal Arch

See Arc de Triomf

University   J 5 and C–D 9–10

As early as the end of the 13th c. the Dominican monks in Barcelona provided educational facilities in the form of a "Studium Generale", and in 1401 institutions were established for the study of medicine and the fine arts, theology, law and philosophy being added a little later. However, following the annulment by Philip V of the special privileges granted to Catalonia, the academy was closed down in 1717. It was 1837 before teaching returned to Barcelona.

At present the University of Barcelona has some 58,000 registered students. For further information on higher education in the city see Introduction, Culture.

From the southern corner of the Plaça de Catalunya the busy shopping street of Carrer del Pelai continues westward to the Plaça de la Universitaria. Here stand the buildings of the Old University, constructed between

Old University

The Zona Universitaria, educational centre of the region

1863 and 1873 in a pseudo-Romanesque style. Inside can be seen two beautiful air-wells and parts of the university library.

Zona Universitaria

Some way out, at the south-western end of the Avinguda de la Diagonal, the extensive modern campus of the Zona Universitaria spreads over the Pedralbes (see entry) district of the city. It is here that the natural science and social and economic science faculties of the university are situated.

Waxworks

See Museu de Cera

*Zoo

L 3 · d 1

Location
Parc de la
Ciutadella

Metro
Ciutadella (L4)

Open
Daily 10am–5pm in
winter;
9.30am–7.30pm in
summer

The Zoo was founded in 1892, and covers some 14 hectares/35 acres of the eastern part of the Parc de la Ciutadella (see entry). An astonishing amount of skill and imagination has gone into creating such a varied and wide-ranging layout in the smallest of spaces.

Among the apes special mention should be made of "Floquet de Neu" ("Snowflake"), a giant white gorilla, the only one in captivity.
Very well laid out are the reptile house and, in particular, the aquarama (dolphinarium), which also houses a giant killer whale, orcinus orca. The circular pool is surrounded by the two-storey aquarium, with salt water on the upper level and fresh water below; the dolphinarium can be viewed through reinforced glass.
The bird house with a separate section for nocturnal birds is also well designed.

There are a number of refreshment stalls and picnic tables, some near the centrally located model of Montserrat (see entry). The skeleton of a large whale is on open display. It is easy to find the way around, as there are coloured symbols on all the pathways indicating the various sections.

Original in concept is the well-known statue of the "Senyoreta del Paraigua" ("Lady with the Umbrella").

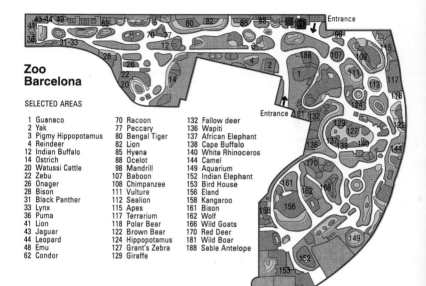

Zoo
Barcelona

SELECTED AREAS

1 Guanaco	70 Racoon	132 Fallow deer
2 Yak	77 Peccary	136 Wapiti
3 Pigmy Hippopotamus	80 Bengal Tiger	137 African Elephant
4 Reindeer	82 Lion	138 Cape Buffalo
12 Indian Buffalo	85 Hyena	140 White Rhinoceros
14 Ostrich	88 Ocelot	144 Camel
20 Watussi Cattle	98 Mandrill	149 Aquarium
22 Zebu	107 Baboon	152 Indian Elephant
26 Onager	108 Chimpanzee	153 Bird House
28 Bison	111 Vulture	156 Eland
31 Black Panther	112 Sealion	158 Kangaroo
33 Lynx	115 Apes	161 Bison
36 Puma	117 Terrarium	162 Wolf
41 Lion	118 Polar Bear	166 Wild Goats
43 Jaguar	122 Brown Bear	170 Red Deer
44 Leopard	124 Hippopotamus	181 Wild Boar
48 Emu	127 Grant's Zebra	188 Sable Antelope
62 Condor	129 Giraffe	

© Baedeker

139

Practical Information

Air Travel

Barcelona airport is situated about 12km/7½ miles south-west of the city in El Prat de Llobregat, close to the motorway (C244) to Castelldefels, RENFE, the state railway company, operates connecting services to the city centre (Sants station; stopping at El Clot, Arc de Triompf, Plaça de Catalunya and Sants Estació) every 30 minutes between 7am and 11pm, journey time 16 minutes. There are also buses (lines EA and EN to the Plaça d'Espanya) and taxis. Since the summer of 1989 the airport has been undergoing extensive modernisation.

Airport

Airlines

Passeig de Gràcia 59
E–08007 Barcelona
tel. 2 15 21 12

British Airways

Passeig de Gràcia 30
E–08007 Barcelona
tel. 3 01 39 93

Iberia

Most other airlines serving Barcelona have desks at the airport.

Bullfighting

In Barcelona bullfights are held on almost every Sunday and public holidays from Easter to November and sometimes also on weekdays (particularly Thursdays). They take place between 4 and 6 or between 5 and 7 in the afternoons, but only in good weather. During the dog days (July–August) and from mid-October onwards only the lesser forms of bullfighting, known as *novilladas*, with less experienced bullfighters and young bulls, are held.
For further information on bullfighting see Facts and Figures, Customs and Traditions.

The bullring Plaça de Toros Monumental is situated south-west of the Plaça de les Glòries Catalanes.

Camping

More than two-thirds of all Spanish camp sites are situated in the autonomous region of Catalonia and here they are concentrated in the area near the coast. The equipment of the sites is considerably above the average for the country; the sites are divided officially into four categories designated L (luxury), 1, 2 and 3.

General

Every camp site provides safe keeping for articles of value; it is advisable to deposit with them large sums of money and valuables.

◀ *A street in the Poble Espanyol – a taste of Andalusia*

In the case of justified complaints the visitor should demand the *Hoja de Reclamaciones*, a form which the owner of the site must hand over on demand. The original of the completed form is sent to the provincial office of the Catalonian regional administration or to the State Secretary for Tourism (Secretaria del Estado del Turismo, Calle de Maria de Molina 50, E–28006 Madrid).

Spending one night in a caravan or motor caravan in lay-bys and car parks is allowed but not on the open roads. Camping away from recognised sites is frowned upon, not least because of the danger of forest and heath fires breaking out in the dry months of the year.

Warning for drivers towing caravans and motor caravan drivers

Through roads usually avoid the old centres of the mountain and coastal resorts. Drivers towing caravans and drivers of motorised caravans are advised to avoid the temptation of entering the centre of these places as often the streets are so narrow that traffic jams are likely to occur.

List of camp sites

Every year the national or regional authorities publish lists of officially recognised camp sites; these can be obtained from information offices (see Information).

Camp site in Barcelona

Camping Cala Gogó
E–08820 El Prat de Llobregat
This site is close to the airport so it can be quite noisy. The quality of the sea water is not of the usual standard.

Camp sites in the area

Camping Masnou
E–08320 El Masnou (15km/9 miles north-east)

Camping Ballena Alegre
E–08840 Villadecans (15km/9 miles south-west)

Camping Tres Estrellas and Camping Albatros
E–08850 Gavá (20km/12 miles south-west)

Car Rental

Avis

Carrer Rita Bonnat 5
(in Les Corts district)
E–08029 Barcelona
tel. 3 79 40 26 and 4 24 84 99

Carrer Casanova 209
(in Sarrià district)
E–08021 Barcelona
tel. 2 09 95 33

Carrer Aragó 235
(in Eixample district)
E–08007 Barcelona
tel. 2 15 84 30

Barcelona Airport
(in El Prat de Llobregat)
E–08820 Barcelona
tel. 2 41 14 76 and 3 29 62 45

Budget

Avinguda Roma 15
(in Eixample district)
E–08029 Barcelona
tel. 3 22 90 12

Carrer Vilodomat
(in Eixample district)
E–08029 Barcelona
tel. 4 39 84 03 and 4 39 84 01

Carrer Consell de Cent 363
(in Eixample district)
E–08009 Barcelona
tel. 3 17 58 76 and 3 17 57 03

Sants Railway Station
(in Sants/Montjuïc district)
E–08014 Barcelona
tel. 4 90 86 62

Carrer Tusset 10
(in Sarrià/Sant Gervasi district)
E–08006 Barcelona
tel. 2 37 37 37

Barcelona Airport
(in El Prat de Llobregat)
E–08820 El Prat
tel. 2 41 13 81 and 3 70 57 52

Europcar

Hertz

Currency

The unit of currency is the peseta (pta). There notes in denominations of 500, 1000, 2000, 5000 and 10,000 pesetas and coins for 1, 5, 10, 25, 50, 100, 200 and 500 pesetas.

Current exchange rates can be found in national newspapers and may be obtained from banks and tourist offices.

Exchange rates (subject to fluctuation)

There are no restrictions on the import of Spanish or foreign currency (cash or cheques). It is advisable, however, to declare large sums of foreign currency (over the equivalent of 500,000 ptas).
There is a limit of 100,000 ptas on the amount of Spanish currency that may be exported. The export of foreign currency is permitted up to the equivalent of 500,000 ptas, or a larger sum if declared on entry.

Import and export of currency

Outside the opening hours of banks (Mon.–Fri. 9am–2pm, Sat. 9am–12.30 or 1pm) money can be changed in exchange offices and travel agencies and at the reception desk of the larger hotels. Money is changed at the official rate, but a varying rate of commission may be charged.

Banks Exchange

It is advisable to take money in the form of Eurocheques or travellers' cheques.
A Eurocheque book and card must be obtained from a bank (charge from £4–£8 for the card and 30p to £1.95 per cheque). Some banks impose a 1.6% commission and/or a handling fee. Eurocheques can be drawn for amounts up to £100 in local currency.

Eurocheques, etc.

Most of the international credit cards are accepted by banks and by many hotels, restaurants and shops.

Credit cards

Holders of Eurocheque cards can draw cash from more than 4500 Eurocheque cash dispensers in Spain. Holders of credit cards (Visa, Access, American Express, etc.) can also draw cash from dispensers bearing the appropriate symbol. American Express has more than 150 of its own dispensers which will issue travellers' cheques as well as cash.

Cash dispensers

Customs Regulations

Loss of cards   The loss of a Eurocheque card or credit card should be reported at once by telephone to the issuing organisation. The major credit card companies have emergency branches in Madrid.

American Express	91–5 72 03 03 and 91–2 79 62 00
Diner's Club	91–2 47 40 00
Visa	91–4 35 24 45 and 91–4 35 30 40

Customs Regulations

Entry from EC countries
In addition to personal effects the following items can be imported into Spain duty-free by visitors over 17: 1 litre of spirits over 22° proof or 2 litres under 22° proof, plus 2 litres of table wine; 200 cigarettes or 100 cigarillos or 50 cigars or 250 grammes of tobacco; 50 cl perfume and $\frac{1}{4}$ litre toilet water. In addition visitors over 15 can import gifts to the value of 5000 pesetas (2000 pesetas for those under 15). Higher limits apply for items obtained duty- and tax-paid in EC countries.

For expensive items such as video equipment, portable radios and televisions an amount equivalent to their value may be payable in customs duty. Information on regulations concerning the importation of hunting rifles and ammunition is available from the Spanish consulates (see Diplomatic Representation).

Entry from non-EC countries
The duty-free allowance is as for EC countries except that the tobacco allowance is doubled.

Diplomatic Representation

United Kingdom
Consulate
Avinguda Diagonal 477
Edificio Torre de Barcelona, 13th floor
E–08036 Barcelona. Tel. 3 22 21 51

Ireland
Consulate
Cran Via Carles III 94
E–08028 Barcelona. Tel.l 3 30 96 52

United States
Consulate
Via Laietana 33
E–08003 Barcelona. Tel. 3 19 95 50

Canada
Consulate
Via Augusta 125
E–08006 Barcelona. Tel. 2 09 06 34

Emergencies

Municipal Police	Emergency number of Policía Municipal	092
National Police	Emergency number of Policía Nacional	091
Fire Brigade	Emergency number of Bomberos (Fire Brigade)	080

Ambulance service of Creu Roja (Red Cross)	3 00 20 20	Red Cross
Reial Automòbil Club de Catalunya	2 00 07 55	R.A.C.C. Breakdown service
Emergency doctor service (Médicos de Urgencia)	2 55 55 55	Doctor

Events

Cavalcades dels Reis Mags (Three Kings' Day processions; January 4th and 5th)
Festa Major del Barri de Sant Antoni (city district festival; middle of the month)
Start of Monte Carlo Rally for Spanish competitors (end of the month)

January

Setmana del Llibre Català (Catalan Book Week; beginning of the month)
Carnestoltes (Carnival; in all districts)
Festa de Santa Eulàlia (festival of the city's patron saint; February 12th)

February

Setmana Santa (Holy Week; processions)
Festa de Sant Medir (Gràcia district festival; beginning of the month) Ralli Internacional de Cotxes d'època (Barcelona – Sitges veteran car rally)

March

Setmana del Llibre (Book Week; in the Poble Espanyol)
Setmana Internacional de Música Contemporània (Week of Contemporary Music)
Diada de Sant Jordi (St George's Day; book and rose festival, April 23rd)
Festa Major del Barri de la Sagrada Familia (city district festival)

April

Fira del Llibre (Book trade fair; end of the month)
Fira de Sant Ponç (traditional honey market; in the Old Town, May 11th)
Festas de Maig al Districte de Sant Marti (city district festival; beginning of the month)
Festivitat de Santa Rita (rose and candle market; in the Old Town)
District festivals in Sarrià-Sant Gervasi, Sant Andreu, Horta, etc.

May

Festa Major de Ciutat Meridiana (Nouse Barris district festival; middle of the month)
Revetiles de Sant Joan (Midsummer Night festival; in all districts; June 23rd and 24th)
District festivals in the Old Town, in Sants-Montjuïc, Sarrià-Sant Gervasi, horta, etc.
Festival Internacional del Cinema (international film festival)
Festival Grec (cultural festival; early June to early August)

June

Beneddicció de Cotxes per Sant Cristòfol (Festival of St Christopher; blessing of vehicles)
Processó Marinera de la Verge del Carme (district festival with procession near the harbour)
District festivals in Horta, Nous Barris and the Old Town
A Nous Barris Marxa (film and music festival in Nous Barris district; until the end of the month)

July

Festa Major de Sant Roc (St Roch festival in the Old Town; middle of the month)
District festivals in Gràcia, Sants-Montjuïc, Vallvidrera and Sant Marti

August

Excursions

September   Jornades Internacionals de Cant Coral (international choir festival in Museu Marítim)
Festa de Treball (labour festival on Montjuïc; middle of the month)
Festivitat de la Mercè (festival of the city's patroness; week of September 24th)
Festa Major del Port (harbour festival; middle of the month)
District festivals in Guineueta, Sarrià-San Gervasi, Barceloneta, Horta, Sant Marti, Gràcia, Sant Andreu, Sants-Montjuïc and in the Old Town.
Formula I motor racing on the Circuit de Catalunya (end of the month)

October   Festival de Tardor de Barcelona (festival of theatre, music and dance)
Festa de la Hispanitat (anniversary of the discovery of America; October 12th)
Festivals in all districts
Ralli Vehicles Històrics (vintage car rally)

November   Festa de la Música Catalana (festival of Catalan music; end of the month)
Festa de Tots Sants (All Saints)
Festes de Tardor (autumn festivals; in all districts)
Festa dels Músics – Santa Cecilia (music festival; around November 22nd)
Festival Internacional de Jazz (international jazz festival; all November)

December   Dia de la Constitució (day of the constitution; December 6th)
Fira de Sant Llúcia (crib far in the vicinity of the cathedral; from December 13th)
Festivitat de Sant Esteve (Feast of St Stephen; December 26th)

Excursions

The most important places in the neighbourhood (Costa Dorada, Montseny, Montserrat, Sant Cugat) can be found under a main heading in the A–Z section of this guide.

The following recommended destinations are a little further afield.

Empúries   The excavation site of the ancient town of Emporion, nowadays Empúries, lies on the Golf de Roses, about 130km/80 miles north-east of Barcelona. it was founded in the 6th c. B.C. by Greek settlers, coming under Roman rule in the 3rd c. B.C. and was destroyed by the Frankish-Alemannic armies in the 3rd c. A.D.
The ruins are made up of the Greek lower town and the Roman upper town. The site comprises extensive remains of various buildings, mosaic floors and large water cisterns together with an interesting museum. In the Roman upper town, which has still only been partly excavated, there are mosaic floors, a surrounding wall and the limited remains of an amphitheatre.

Figueres   Figueres is about 15km/9 miles inland from the Golf de Roses. It is the birthplace of the Surrealist artist and sculptor Salvador Dali. The principal attraction is the Museu Salvador Dali which is accommodated in a former theatre and contains a fascinating collection of works by this exceptional artist.

Girona   Girona, the capital of the province of the same name, is about 90km/56 miles from Barcelona either on the motorway which leads to the Spanish-French border or on the national road which runs parallel along the Costa

Dorada. It is situated at the confluence of the Riu Onyar and the Riu Ter and has an impressive old-world old Town, a Gothic cathedral (fine cloisters) and other ecclesiastical buildings. The Cathedral Museum houses exhibits of Romanesque and Gothic church architecture; of particular interest is the colourful wall tapestry (11th c.) depicting the history of the Creation. The Passeig Arqueològic (Paseo Arqueológico), a marked archeological walk, takes in the most important sites of the Old Town.

The national road 152 leads north to the provincial towm of Ripoll in the valley of the above-mentioned Riu Ter about 90km/56 miles from Barcelona and 50km/31 miles south of the state boundary on the Collado de Ares. In the principal square in the heart of the town centre stands the large complex of buildings which belong to the Benedictine monastery of Santa Maria. The monastery was completely rebuilt to the same design after being destroyed by fire. The most significant relic is the magnificent main doorway (12th c.) of the Romanesque church. It is notable for the great number of representations of themes of the Old and New Testaments. The cloisters (12th–15th c.) are also noteworthy.

Ripoll

Not far to the east of Ripoll a minor road leads to Sant Joan de la Abadesses with the Romanesque church of Saint Joan (12th c.) which formerly belonged to a monastery. It houses a carved group depicting the Descent from the Cross (12th c.) and has interesting cloisters and a museum.

Sant Joan de les Abadesses

The road from Sant Joan continues to the beautifully situated ruins of the former Benedictine monastery of Sant Pere de Rodes, one of the most important examples of Romanesque architecture in Catalonia.

Sant Pere de Rodes

On the estuarine plain of the Riu Ter east of Girona (see above) is the excavated site of Poblat Ibéric (Iberian settlement c. 7th–2nd c. B.C.), the largest site of its kind in northern Spain. There are extensive remains of the town walls and houses. A museum stands on the acropolis hill.

Ullastret

The route to Ripoll (see above) leads to the bishopric of Vic, 60km/37 miles north of Barcelona. On the edge of the Old Town is the great cathedral (originally founded in 1040; extensively rebuilt 1803–21 and again following the Civil War). In the choir ambulatory a coloured and richly gilded marble altar (15th c.) with scenes from the life of Jesus and St Peter; in the triple-storeyed cloisters (Romanesque, Gothic and Renaissance) is the bombastic monument of Jaime Balmes (1810–48) who was sometime advisor to Pope Pius IX and is considered the most important Spanish academic of the 19th c. The Museu Episcopal, opposite the cathedral, houses an excellent collection of Romanesque ecclesiastical art (sculpture and frescoes) together with Gothic and Baroque art treasures.

Vic

For more information about the region of Catalonia north-east of Barcelona consult the Baedeker guide "Costa Brava".

Food and Drink

Spaniards have always taken their meals much later than other Europeans, (lunch between 1 and 3pm and dinner as late as 9 or even 10pm) though with the development of the tourist trade it is now usually possible to get lunch or dinner rather earlier than in the past.

The normal Spanish breakfast is a very simple meal, but hotels accustomed to catering for foreign visitors, particularly those in the higher categories,

Confectionery to tempt eye and palate

often provide a buffet breakfast offering more substantial fare, which may include a choice of coffee, tea, fruit juice, various kinds of bread, jam, eggs and cold meat.

Spanish meals are usually substantial (hors d'œuvre, etc., followed by main dish, fruit and cheese). The fixed-price menu (*comida*) of four or more courses is considerably cheaper than eating à la carte. The tourist menu, in three price ranges, consists of three courses: the price usually includes a quarter litre of wine or beer, service and other charges.

Spanish cooking makes much use of olive oil (*aceite de oliva*) and garlic (*ajo*). Egg dishes, rice dishes and fish are particularly tasty and appetising. There are many restaurants specialising in seafood (*marisquerías*).

An alternative to a restaurant meal is offered by the *tascas* (bars), which provide a variety of appetisers (*tapas*) – olives, pickled vegetables, kebabs, ham, seafood, garlic potatoes, pieces of tortilla, etc. – often supplied free as an accompaniment to drinks. If you want more you can order a *ración* of the titbits displayed on the counter. In this way, particularly by visiting a number of tascas in the course of the evening, it is possible to make up a substantial and varied meal. An advantage is that the bars are open all the time, while restaurants open only at 9pm and may be full by 10pm. Outside the large tourist centres on the coasts tapas are a very good bargain.

Typical
Spanish dishes

Hors d'œuvres (*entremeses*) include sausage, cold meats, ham (jamón serrano), seafood and olives. A Catalonian speciality is blood sausage or black pudding *butifarra* or *butifarron*.

Among Spanish soups (*sopas*) gazpacho is the best known. Served cold, it is made from tomatoes, cucumber, onions, garlic and peppers with vinegar, oil and spices; the diced vegetables are often served separately.

Bars, popular for snacks

The first main course (*plato fuerte*) is often tortillas (omelettes), in numerous variations both savoury and sweet. The various local dishes combining meat and vegetables are both nourishing and substantial. Among them are *cocido,* a stew of meat, chick peas, bacon, potatoes and other vegetables, the exact composition varying from one part of the country to another. Also excellent when properly made is the well-known *paella,* a rice dish made with chicken, meat, fish, seafood, beans and peas for which Valencia is particularly renowned. It usually has to be ordered for a minimum of two people.

Fish dishes (*pescados*) are a delicacy but are not as abundant as might be expected in a port. *Zarzuela de mariscos* is a stew of different kinds of fish, highly seasoned. Fish are also served as *tapas* (appetisers), particularly eels (*anguilas*) boiled in oil with garlic and pepper. Any kind of fresh fish is excellent simply fried in oil.

Spain has a great variety of desserts (*postres*) – excellent cheeses and a wide range of sweets. *Turrón* (a kind of nougat made with honey and almonds) and marzipan date from Moorish times; and in addition there are pastries (*ensaimadas),* spiced cakes, flan (caramel custard), candied yolk of egg and magnificent fruit.

The preferred Spanish drink is wine. Ordinary table wine (*vino corriente* or *vino de mesa*) is frequently mixed with water or mineral water. For further information on Catalonian wine-production see Wine.

Drinks (bebidas)

Sangria, a popular refreshing drink, is a mixture of red wine, brandy, mineral water and orange and lemon juice with cubes of fruit and ice.

Beer (*cerveza*) is becoming increasingly popular in Spain. Beer restaurants (*cervecerías*) serve imported beers as well as the lighter Spanish beers.

149

Food and Drink

Non-alcoholic drinks include a variety of fruit juices as well as mineral water (*con gas* = sparkling; *sin gas* = still). Spanish water is usually heavily chlorinated; a pleasanter drink is spring water, which is not expensive (sold in plastic containers, usually of 5 litres).

Spanish brandy (*brandy, coñac*) is a popular drink. To get the full aroma it should be ordered in a warmed glass (*vaso caliente*). This can become quite a ceremony: the waiter warms the glass over a spirit stove, pours in a little brandy and swills it round in the glass over the flame until the alcoholic vapours ignite and fill the glass with a pale blue flame; he then pours in more brandy, which diffuses a rich aroma.

Reading the Spanish Menu

Miscellaneous	cubierto	table-setting, cutlery
	cuchara	spoon
	cucharita	teaspoon
	cuchillo	knife
	tenedor	fork
	plato	plate
	vaso	glass
	taza	cup
	servilleta	napkin
	sacacorchos	corkscrew
	bocadillo	sandwich
	butifarra	Catalan sausage
	chorizo	red paprika sausage
	torreznos	rashers of bacon
Meals	desayuno	breakfast
	comida	lunch
	cena	dinner
Hors d'œuvre (entremeses)	aceitunas	olives
	ensalada	salad
	ostras	oysters
	anchoas	anchovies
	sardinas	sardines
	jamón	ham
	rábanos	radishes
	mantequilla	butter
	pan	bread
	panecillo	roll
	sopa de legumbres (de yerbas, de verduras)	vegetable soup
	sopa con guisantes	pea soup
	sopa de lentejas	lentil soup
	sopa con tomates	tomato soup
	sopa de fideos	noodle soup
	sopa de arroz	rice soup
	sopa de pescado	fish soup
	caldo	bouillon
	gazpacho	cold vegetable soup

huevo	egg	Egg dishes
crudo	raw	(platos de
fresco	fresh	huevos)
duro	hard-boiled	
pasado por agua	soft-boiled	
tortilla	omelette	
huevos revueltos	scrambled eggs	
huevos frites (huevos al plato)	fried eggs	
huevos con tomate	eggs fried with tomato	

frito	fried	Fish (pescado)
asado	roasted	and seafood
cocido	boiled	(mariscos)
ahumado	smoked	
a la plancha	roasted on a griddle	

anguila	eel
arenque	herring
atún	tunny
bacalao	cod
besugo	sea bream
carpa	carp
esturión	sturgeon
gado	haddock
lenguado	sole
merluza	hake
rodaballo	turbot
salmón	salmon
sollo	pike
trucha	trout

almeja	clam
bogavante	lobster
calamar	squid
camarón	shrimp, prawn
cangrejo de mar	crab
cangrejo de río	crayfish
gamba	prawn
langosta	spiny lobster
ostras	oysters

asado	roast	Meat
carne ahumada	smoked meat	(carnes)
carne estofada	stew	
carne salada	salt meat	
chuleta	chop, cutlet	
fiambre	cold meat	
jamón	ham	
serrano	smoked	
salchichón	salami-type sausage	

bistec	steak
buey	beef
carnero	mutton
cerdo	pork
cochinillo, lechón	sucking pig
cordero	lamb
rosbif	roast beef

Food and Drink

	ternera	veal
	tocino	bacon
	vaca	beef
Poultry (aves)	faisán	pheasant
	ganso	goose
	pato	duck
	perdiz	partridge
	pichón	pigeon
	pollo	chicken
Game (caza)	ciervo	venison (red deer)
	corzo	roe-deer
	jabalí	wild boar
	liebre	hare
Vegetables (verduras)	alcachofas	artichokes
	apio	celery
	cebollas	onions
	col de Bruselas	Brussels sprouts
	coliflor	cauliflower
	col lombarda	red cabbage
	ensalada	salad
	escarola	endive
	espárragos	asparagus
	espinacas	spinach
	garbanzos	chick peas
	guisantes	peas
	judías	beans
	lechuga	lettuce
	patatas	potatoes
	patatas fritas	chips
	pepinillo	gherkin
	pepino	cucumber
	pepollo	cabbage
	tomates	tomatoes
	zanahorias	carrots
Condiments (condimentos)	aceite	oil
	mostaza	mustard
	pimienta	pepper
	sal	salt
	vinagre	vinegar
Desserts (postres)	barquillos	wafers
	bollo	bun
	compota	compote
	dulces	sweets
	flan	caramel cream
	helado	ice
	de chocolate	chocolate ice
	de frambuesa	raspberry ice
	de vainilla	vanilla ice
	con nata	with whipped cream
	membrillo	quince jelly
	pastel	cake
	queso	cheese
	tarta	tart
	torrijas	fritters

cerezas	cherries	Fruit
chumbos	prickly pears	(frutas)
dátiles	dates	
fresas	strawberries	
higos	figs	
limón	lemon	
mandarinas	mandarines	
manzana	apple	
melocotón	peach	
melones	melons	
naranjas	oranges	
nueces	walnuts	
pera	pear	
piña	pineapple	
plátano	banana	
uvas	grapes	
agua mineral	mineral water (con gas = carbonated; sin gas = still)	Drinks
cerveza	beer (dorada = light; negra = dark)	
café con leche	white coffee	
café helado	iced coffee	
café solo	black espresso coffee	
horchata	refreshing almond drink	
jugo	juice	
té	tea	
vino	wine (blanco = white; tinto = red; rosado = rosé)	
See entry		Restaurants
See entry		Wine

Getting to Barcelona

Because of the distance between Britain and Spain it is advisable to allow three days for the journey making two overnight stops, although it can be done comfortably by experienced motorists in two days. The mileage can be reduced by using one of the motor-rail services which will take the visitor and his vehicle at least part of the way to Spain; information can be obtained from French Railways, 179 Piccadilly, London WIV OBA (tel. 071 409 3518). It should be pointed out that the motorways in France and Spain are subject to tolls.

By car

Barcelona airport is situated to the south-west of the city in El Prat de Llobregat. The Spanish National Airline Iberia and British Airways fly direct from London to Barcelona. Scheduled services between North America and Spain are provided by Iberia, TWA and Canadian Pacific Airlines either direct or via London. There are flight connections, sometimes with a stop-over, from all major European airports. Iberia and its affiliate Aviaco operate flights between Barcelona and other Spanish cities.

By air

There are through services from Paris to Barcelona usually travelling overnight; it is possible to leave London late in the morning, change in Paris and travel by the Barcelona Talgo train departing Paris (Austerlitz) at 9pm and arriving in Barcelona about 8.30 the following morning.
For further information see Railways and Railway Stations.

By train

Hotels

General

Hotels in Spain are officially classified in various categories according to their function and standard hoteles (singular hotel) providing accommodation with or without meals usually with their own restaurant; hoteles apartamentos: apartment hotels with facilities similar to hotels but with accommodation in flats or bungalows (chalets); hostales (singular hostal) modest hotels or inns providing accommodation with or without meals; pensiones (singular pensión) pensions or guest houses with a limited number of rooms, providing full board only.

Hotels, apartment hotels and hostales may also be run as residencias, providing only accommodation and usually breakfast.

Hotel Categories

Official	In this book
*****	L (luxury)
****	I
***	II
**	III
*	IV

Luxury hotels in the following list are additionally designated by a red star.

Hostales and
pensiones

***	PI
**	PII
*	PIII

Hotel lists

The Spanish Ministry of Traffic, Tourism and Communications publishes annually a list of hotels and apartments. Also, particularly for the individual autonomous provinces such as Barcelona, lists can be obtained from the Spanish Tourist Information Office (see Information).

Hotels in Barcelona (selection)

*Ritz, Gran Via de les Corts Catalanes 668, L, 161 r.
*Avenida Palace, Gran Via de les Corts Catalanes 605, L, 211 r.
*Diplomatic, Carrer Pau Claris 122, L, 213 r.
*Melià Barcelona Sarrià, Avinguda de Sarrià 50, L, 312 r.
*Presidente, Avinguda de la Diagonal 570, L, 161 r.
*Princesa Sofía, Plaça Pius XII 4, L, 504 r.
*Ramada Renaissance Barcelona, Ramblas 111, L, 209 r.
Alexandra, Carrer de Mallorca 251, I, 75 r.
Arenas (no rest.), Carrer Capità Arenas 20, I, 59 r.
Balmoral (no rest.), Via Augusta 5, I, 94 r.
Barcelona (no rest.), Carrer Casp 1–13, I, 64 r.
Colón, Avinguda de la Catedral 7, I 155 r.
Comtes de Barcelona, Passeig de Gràcia 75, I, 100 r.
Condor (no rest.), Via Augusta 127, I, 78 r.
Cristal (no rest.), Carrer de la Diputació 257, I, 148 r.
Dante (no rest.), Carrer de Mallorca 181, I, 81 r.
Derby (no rest.), Carrer Loreto 21, I, 116 r.
Ducs de Bergara, Carrer Bergara 11, I, 56 r.
Gran Hotel Calderón (no rest.), Rambla de Catalunya 26, I, 244 r.
Gran Hotel Cristina (no rest.), Avinguda de la Diagonal 458, I, 123 r.
Hesperia (no rest.), Els Vergós 20, I, 139 r.
Majéstic, Passeig de Gràcia 70, I, 336 r.
Master, Carrer de València 105, I, 81 r.
Núñez-Urgel (no rest.), Carrer Comte d'Urgell 232, I, 121 r.

Regente, Rambla de Catalunya 76, I, 78 r.
Rívoli Ramblas, Rambla dels Estudis 128, I, 87 r.
Roma, Avinguda Roma 31, I, 42 r.
Royal (no rest.), Ramblas 117, I, 108 r.

Aragón (no rest.), Carrer de Aragón 569, II, 72 r.
Astoria (no rest.), Carrer de Paris 203, II, 108 r.
Atenas, Avinguda Meridiana 151, II, 166 r.
Belagua, Via Augusta 89, II, 72 r.
Castellnou, Carrer Castellnou 61, II, 29 r.
Condado, Carrer Aribau 201, II, 89 r.
Covadonga (no rest.), Avinguda de la Diagonal 596, II, 76 r.
Expo Hotel (no rest.), Carrer de Mallorca 1–23, II, 432 r.
Ficus (no rest.), Carrer de Mallorca 163, II, 74 r.
Fornos (no rest.), Ramblas 44, II, 30 r.
Gaudí, Carrer Nou de la Rambla 12, II, 71 r.
Gótico (no rest.), Carrer Jaume I 14, II, 72 r.
Gran Via, Gran Via de les Corts Catalanes 642, II, 48 r.
Gravina (no rest.), Carrer Gravina 12, II, 60 r.
Habana (no rest.), Gran Via de les Corts Catalanes 647, II, 65 r.
Les Corts (no rest.), Travessera de les Corts 292, II, 80 r.
Metropol, Carrer Ample 31, II, 68 r.
Mitre (no rest.), Carrer Bertran 9–15, II, 57 r.
Moderno, Carrer del Hospital 11, II, 52 r.
Montecarlo (no rest.), Rambla Estudios 124, II, 73 r.
Numància (no rest.), Carrer de Numància 74, II, 142 r.
Oriente, Ramblas 45–47, II, 142 r.
Pedralbes, Carrer Fontcoberta 4, II, 28 r.
Rallye (no rest.), Travessera de les Corts 150, II, 73 r.
Regencia Colón (no rest.), Carrer Sagristans 13–17, II, 55 r.
Regina, Carrer Bergara 2, II, 102 r.
Rialto (no rest.), Carrer Ferran 40–42, II, 128 r.
Suizo, Plaça de l'Angel 12, II, 50 r.
Terminal (no rest.), Carrer de Provença 1, II, 75 r.
Tres Torres (no rest.), Carrer Calatrava 32–34, II, 56 r.
Villa de Madrid (no rest.), Plaça Vila de Madrid 3, II, 28 r.
Wilson (no rest.), Avinguda de la Diagonal 568, II, 52 r.
Zenit (no rest.), Carrer Santaló 8, II, 61 r.

Antibes (no rest.), Carrer de la Diputació 394, III, 65 r.
Auto Hogar (no rest.), Avinguda Paral.lel 64, III, 156 r.
Bonanova Park (no rest.), Carrer Capitá Arenas 51, III, 60 r.
Catalunya (no rest.), Carrer Santa Anna 22, III, 40 r.
Cortes (no rest.), Carrer Santa Anna 25, III, 46 r.
España, Carrer Sant Pau 9–11, III, 84 r.
Flor Park (no rest.), Ramblas Capuchinas 57, III, 30 r.
L'Alguer (no rest.), Carrer Pére Rodríguez 20, III, 33 r.
Lleó, Carrer Pelai 24, III, 42 r.
Mesón de Castilla (no rest.), Carrer Valldonzella 5, III, 56 r.
Principal (no rest.), Carrer Junta del Comerç 8, III, 55 r.
Ravisol, Passatge Bacardi 1, III, 28 r.
San Agustín, Plaça de Sant Agustí 3, III, 71 r.
Via Augusta (no rest.), Via Augusta 63, III, 52 r.

Apolo (no rest.), Ramblas 33, IV, 90 r.
Centro (no rest.), Carrer Sant Pau 2, IV, 28 r.
Climent (no rest.),Gran Via de les Corts Catalanes 304, IV, 35 r.
Coronado (no rest.), Carrer Nou de la Rambla 134, IV, 26 r.
Cosmos (no rest.), Carrer Escudellers 19, IV, 67 r.
Ginebra, Rambla de Catalunya 1, IV, 10 r.
Inglés (no rest.), Carrer de la Boquería 17, IV, 29 r.

Information

Internacional (no rest.), Ramblas 78, IV, 59 r.
Lloret (no rest.), Rambla Canaletas 125, IV, 53 r.
Monegal (no rest.), Carrer Pelai 62, IV, 23 r.
Nouvel (no rest.), Carrer Santa Anna 18–20, IV, 76 r.
Park Hotel, Avinguda Marquès de l'Argentera 11, IV, 95 r.
Sans (no rest.), Carrer Antoni de Capmany 82, IV, 76 r.
Santa Marta, Carrer General Castaños 14, IV, 65 r.
Transit, Carrer Rector Triadó 82, IV, 27 r.

Information

In the United Kingdom

London

Spanish Tourist Office
57–58 St James's Street
London SW1A 1LD
Tel. (071) 499 0901 and (071) 499 1169

In Canada

Toronto

Tourist Office of Spain
102 Bloor Street West, 14th floor
Toronto, Ont. M5S IM8
Tel. (416) 961 3131 and (416) 961 4079

in the United States

New York

Tourist Office of Spain
665 Fifth Avenue
New York, NY 10022
Tel. (212) 759 8822

Chicago

Tourist Office of Spain
Water Tower Place, Suite 951 East
845 N. Michigan Avenue
Chicago, IL 60611
Tel. (312) 642 1992, (312) 944 0216 and (312) 944 0225–6

Miami

Tourist Office of Spain
1221 Brickell Avenue
Miami, Fl 33131
Tel. (305) 358 1992

Los Angeles

Spanish Tourist Office
8383 Wilshire Blvd., Suite 960
Beverly Hills
Los Angeles, CA 90211
Tel. (213) 658 7188 and 658 7191/92/95

In Barcelona

Patronat Municipal
de Turisme

Head Office:
Passeig de Gràcia 35
E–08007 Barcelona
Tel. 2 15 44 77
(for specialised information)

General Information Bureaux
Sants Station
E–08003 Barcelona
Tel. 4 10 25 94

Moll de la Fusta (harbour)
E–08002 Barcelona
Tel. 4 12 26 40

Feira de Barcelona (Trade Fair Complex)
Plaça de l'Univers
E–08004 Barcelona
Tel. 3 25 52 35
(only open during trade fairs and exhibitions)

Town Hall
Plaça de Sant Jaume
E–08002 Barcelona
Tel. 3 18 25 25 (summer only)

Gran Via de les Corts Catalanes 658
E–08010 Barcelona
Tel. 3 01 74 43 (closed on Sundays)

El Prat Airport
E–08820 El Prat de Llobregat
Tel. 3 25 58 29

For visitors with a professional interest information regarding access to   Càtedra Gaudí
certain parts of this modernist building which are not usually open to the
public is available from the Finca Güell (see A–Z).

Càtedra Gaudí
Avinguda Pedralbes 7
E–08034 Barcelona
Tel. 2 04 52 50

Insurance

Visitors are strongly advised to ensure that they have adequate holiday   General
insurance, including loss or damage to luggage, loss of currency and
jewellery.

Residents of other European Community countries may receive medical   Health
care when on holiday in Spain on production of a form issued by their
national health service (form E111 for British citizens). Treatment can be
obtained free of charge, but up to 40% of the cost of prescribed medicines
must be paid, except for pensioners who are exempt. A Spanish doctor
must be shown the original form, plus a copy which is retained each time
treatment is sought. therefore a number of photocopies should be taken.
It is essential for visitors from non-EC countries. and advisable for EC
nationals, to take out some form of short-term health insurance providing
complete cover and possibly avoiding delays. Nationals of non-EC countries should certainly have insurance cover.

Visitors travelling by car should be ensure that their insurance is compre-   Vehicles
hensive and covers use of the vehicle in Spain.

See also Travel Documents.

Language

The official language of Spain is Castilian (Castillano) Spanish but most
inhabitants of Barcelona prefer to use Catalan (Català), although Castilian
is widely understood. Place names on signs in the city are almost invariably
in Catalan. In information offices, hotels and restaurants English is generally understood, but even a slight knowledge of Spanish will prove bene-
ficial and the introduction of a word or phrase in Catalan will be greeted
with pleasure. Below are some everyday words and expressions in Castilian ("High" Spanish) and in Catalan:

English	Spanish	Catalan
good morning	Buenos días	bon dia
good day (after midday)	buenas tardes	bona tarda
good night	buenas noches	bona nit
goodbye	adiós/hasta la vista	adéu/passi-ho bé
yes/no	sí/no	sí/no
excuse me	perdón	perdó
don't mention it/ not at all	de nada	de res
help yourself	sírvase usted	serveixi vostè
if you please	por favor	si us plau
thank you (very much)	(muchas) gracias	(moltes) gràcies
allow me	con permiso	amb permis
do you speak English?	¿habla usted inglés?	parla vosté anglès?
I don't understand	no entiendo	no ho entenc
have you a room free	¿hay una habitación libre?	tenen una habitació lliure?
single room	habitación individual	habitació individual
double room	habitación doble	habitació doble
a bath/shower	baño/ducha	bany/dutxa
key	llave	clau
what does it cost?	¿cuánto vale?	quant costa?
the bill/check	cuenta	compte
where is the road . . .?	¿dónde está la calle . . .?	on és el carrer . . .?
street (in a town)	calle	carrer
road (outside a town)	carretera	carretera
motorway/highway	autopista	autopista
to the right	a la derecha	a la dreta
to the left	a la izquierda	a l'esquerra
straight ahead	derecho	dret
above/up	arriba	a dalt
below/down	abajo	a baix
January	enero	gener
February	febrero	febrer
March	marzo	març
April	abril	abril
May	mayo	maig
June	junio	juny
July	julio	juliol
August	agosto	agost
September	setiembre	setembre

October	octubre	octubre
November	noviembre	novembre
December	diciembre	desembre

Monday	lunes	dilluns
Tuesday	martes	dimarts
Wednesday	miércoles	dimecres
Thursday	jueves	dijous
Friday	viernes	divendres
Saturday	sábado	dissabte
Sunday	domingo	diumenge

morning	mañana	matí
midday	mediodía	migdia
evening	tarde	vespre
night	noche	nit

Markets

Almost every district has its municipal market hall with an abundant dis-play of fruit, vegetables, dairy products, meat, fish and seafood. Three of the market halls (Mercat de Born, Mercat de Sant Antoni and Mercat de Sant Josep) are of notable architectural interest; they are described in the A to Z section.

Municipal market halls

In Barcelona there are the following local markets:
Barceloneta (Plaça de la Font), Buen Pastor (Carrer Sant Adrià 154),

Local markets

Mercat de Sant Antoni, the central market on the Ramblas

Canyelles (Carrer Antonio Machado 8), Carmel (Carrer Llobregós – Conca Tremp), Ciutat Meridiana (Carrer Costabona 4), Clot (Plaça Mercat 26), Concepció (Carrer Aragó 317), Encants/Sant Antoni (Carrer Manso-Urgell), Felipe II (Carrer Felip II 118), Fira de Bellcaire (Plaça de les Glòries), Galvany (Carrer Santaló-Madrazo), Guinardó (Passatge Llivia-Oblit), Guineueta (Passeig Valldaura 186), Horta (Carrer Tajo 75), Hostafrancs (Carrer Creu Coberta 93), Les Corts (Travessera de les Corts 229), Lesseps (Carrer Verdi 214), Llibertat (Plaça Llibertat 27), Ninot-Porvenir (Carrer de Mallorca 133), Mare de Déu del Carme (Carrer Cid 10), Mare de Déu la Estrella (Carrer Providència 170), Mare de Déu de la Mercè (Passeig Fabra i Puig 270), Mare de Déu de Montserrat (Via Favència 241), Mare de Déu de Núria (Avinguda Rasos de Peguera 186), Mare de Déu de Port (Carrer Energia 21), Provençals (Carrer Menorca-Treball), Sagrada Familia (Carrer de Mallorca 475), Sagrera (Plaça Masadas 6), Sant Andreu (Plaça Mercadal 41), Sant Antoni (Carrer Comte d'Urgell 1), Sant Gervasi (Plaça Frederic Soler 1), Sant Josep/Boqueria (Rambla Sant Joesep 101), Sant Marti (Carrer Puigcerdà 212), Santa Caterina (Avinguda Francesc Cambó 16), Sants (Carrer Sant Medi 7), Sarriá (Passeig Reina Elisenda de Montcada 7), Tres Torres (Carrer Els Vergós 2), Trinitat (Carrer La Fosca 10), Unión (Plaça de la Unió 25), Vall d'Hebron (Passeig Vall d'Hebron 130) and Vallvidrera (Carrer Reis Catòlics).

Motoring

Driving in Spain

In Spain, as in the rest of continental Europe, traffic travels on the right, with overtaking on the left.

Priority

At junctions and roundabouts traffic coming from the right has priority. This applies even to side streets in towns; exceptions are signposted.

Turning

For left-hand turns off a main road there is often a specially marked filter lane to the right which then turns to cross the main road at right angles.

Overtaking

When overtaking the left-hand indicator must be kept on during the whole process and the right-hand one used when pulling back to the right. The horn must be sounded (or, after dark, the headlights flashed) before overtaking or before a bend. A good lookout should be kept for overtaking lorries. Drivers about to be overtaken should operate their right-hand indicator to show the driver behind that they understand his intention to pass.

Overtaking is prohibited within 100m/110yds of a blind hill and on roads where visibility is less than 200m/220yds.

Lights

On well lit roads (other than expressways or motorways) sidelights alone may be used. Beware of unlit vehicles! It is compulsory for motorcyclists to use dipped headlights during the day.

Motorists in Spain are obliged to carry a spare set of light bulbs.

Traffic Lights

In some instances, when changing from green to red, the green light remains on with the amber. Two red lights, one above the other, indicate no entry.

Parking

Parking is permitted in one-way streets only on the side with even numbers on even-numbered days and on the side with odd numbers on odd-numbered days.

Care is necessary in towns, particularly when the streets are busy in the evening, to avoid pedestrians, who are sometimes reluctant to give way to cars on the roadway. Caution is also required on country roads with relatively little traffic, since country people often pay little heed to the rules of the road.

Pedestrians

Spanish cyclists and motorcyclists often indicate a change of direction by waving an arm up and down, but this does not always make their intention clear: the right arm may be used to give warning of a left turn, or vice versa.

Cyclists

Farm and other animals are often a hazard on country roads. In rural parts of Spain there is often a strip of grazing land alongside the road (even at intersections – a drove road (*cañada*)) for travelling flocks of sheep. A powerful horn is therefore very desirable.

Animals

Foreign motorists in particular should observe strict driving discipline for the sake of their national reputation as well as for their own safety. The directions of the Policia Municipal in towns and the Guardia Civil de Tráfico (traffic police) should be immediately complied with: if a driver fails to stop when signalled to do so the police may well make use of their revolvers, since they are not infrequently on the alert for terrorists. Fines for traffic offences must be paid on the spot, and are high.

Driving discipline

To call the police dial 091 (throughout Spain).
An accident in Spain can have very serious consequences, including the impounding of the car until any legal proceedings have been completed and the detention of the driver pending bail. It is very desirable, therefore, to have a bail bond (see Travel Documents).
An accident should be reported at once to your insurance company in accordance with the instructions on your green card or other insurance document.

Accidents

The towing of broken-down vehicles by private cars is prohibited.

Towing

Speed limits are 120km p.h./74 m.p.h. on motorways, 100km p.h./62 m.p.h on dual carriageways, 90km p.h./56 m.p.h. on other roads and 60km p.h./ 37 m.p.h. in built-up areas. Cars towing trailer caravans are restricted to 80km p.h./49 m.p.h. on motorways and 70km p.h./43 m.p.h. on other roads.

Speed limits

On most motorways (autopista), except some stretches around Madrid and Barcelona, tolls are charged – payable at exit points.

Motorways

The wearing of seat belts both in front and in rear seats is obligatory.

Safety belts

The blood alcohol limit is 0.8 per 1000 (8 milligrams per millilitre).

Alcohol

Standard grade petrol (gasolina normal): 92 octane (not recommended)
Premium grade (gasolina super): 97 octane
Lead-free(sin plomo): 95 octane
Diesel fuel (*gasoleo*) is also available.

Fuel

A spare can containing up to 10 litres (2.2 gallons) can be taken into Spain without payment of duty.

In Catalonia some Catalan spellings are used exclusively on direction signs, but most can be recognised from the Spanish version, e.g. Gerona = Girona, Lérida = Lleida.

Road signs

Spanish Motoring Organisations

RACE

Real Automóvil Club de España (RACE)
Head office:
Calle José Abascal 10
E–28003 Madrid
Tel. (91) 4 47 32 00

Reial Automòbil Club de Catalunya (R.A.C.C.)
Carrer Santaló 8
E–08021 Barcelona
Tel. 2 00 33 11 (2 00 07 55 for 24-hour service)

Breakdown
services

RACE operates a breakdown service. To obtain assistance call the national
breakdown centre in Madrid, tel. 5 93 33 33, which provides a 24-hour
English-speaking service.

R.A.C.C. in Barcelona:
Tel. 91–7 42 12 13 and 91–7 42 98 98

Emergency

Accident (accidente) and breakdown (auxillio en carretera) assistance is
afforded by the Policia Municipal within the city and out of town by the
Guardia Civil de Tráfico.

Emergency
telephones

Emergency (SOS) telephones are sited almost everywhere along the
motorways.

Museums

The most important museums of the city are described in detail in the
"Barcelona from A to Z" section. In addition there are many smaller or
specialist museums for which either prior appointment is necessary or
admission is restricted to specialists.

List of Museums

Casa Museu Gaudí
See A to Z, Parc Güell

Collecció d'Indumentària de Bomber
(Collection of Fire Brigade Uniforms)
Passeig Nacional 67
E–08003 Barcelona
Tel. 3 19 43 53

Fundació Antoni Tàpies
See A to Z

Fundació Joan Miró
See A to Z

Gabinet de Fisica Experimental
See A to Z

Gabinet Numismàtic de Catalunya
See A to Z

Gabinet Postal
See A to Z, Palau de Pedralbes

Galeria de Catalans Illustres
See A to Z

Institute Amatller d'Art Hispànic
(Institute of Spanish Art)
Passeig de Gràcia 41
E–08007 Barcelona
Tel. 2 16 01 75

Institut Botànic
See A to Z

Institut Municipal d'Història
See A to Z

Museu Arqueològic
See A to Z

Museu Automóbil
(Vintage Car Club of Barcelona)
Via Augusta 182
E–08021 Barcelona
Tel. 2 09 55 23

Museu Clarà
See A to Z

Museu d'Art de Catalunya
See A to Z

Museu d'Art Modern
See A to Z

Museu d'Arts Decoratives
See A to Z

Museu d'Arts, Indústries i Tradicions Populars
See A to Z, Poble Espanyol

Museu d'Autòmats
See A to Z, Tibidabo

Museu de Carrosses Fúnebres
(Museum of Funeral Carriages)
Carrer Sancho de Avila 2
E–08018 Barcelona
Tel. 3 00 50 61

Museu de Cera
See A to Z

Museu de Ceràmica
See A to Z

Museu de Geologia
See A to Z

Museu de Geologia del Seminari
(Geological Museum of the Seminari Collection)
Carrer de la Diputacío 231
E–08007 Barcelona
Tel. 2 54 16 00

Museu de la Catedral
See A to Z, Cathedral

Museu de la Ciència
See A to Z

Museu de la Farmàcia Catalana
(Pharmaceutical Museum)
Avinguda Diagonal 643
E–08028 Barcelona
Tel. 3 30 79 20

Museu de la Música
See A to Z

Museu de les Arts de l'Espectacle
See A to Z, Palau Güell

Museu de les Arts Gràfiques
See A to Z, Poble Espanyol

Museu del Foment de Obres i Construccions
(Vehicle collection of the Municipal Department of Works)
Carrer Balmes 36
E–08007 Barcelona
Tel. 3 18 90 00

Museu del Futbol Club Barcelona
See A to Z

Museu de l'Institut de Criminologia
(Criminology Museum of the University Law Faculty)
Avinguda Diagonal 684
E–08034 Barcelona
Tel. 2 05 11 12

Museu del Perfum
See A to Z

Museu del Temple Expiatoria de la Sagrada Familia
See A to Z, Sagrada Familia

Museu de Temàtica Espeleològica
(Cave Museum)
Carrer Maurici Serrahima 19
E–08012 Barcelona
Tel. 2 17 48 02

Museu de Zoologia
See A to Z

Museu d'Història de la Ciutat
See A to Z

Museu d'Història de la Medicina de Catalunya
See A to Z

Museu d'Història del Calçat
See A to Z

Museu d'Holografia
See A to Z

Museu Diocesà
See A to Z

Museu Etnogràfic Andino-Amazònic
See A to Z

Museu Etnològic
See A to Z

Museu Frederic Marès
See A to Z

Museu Gabinet Postal
See A to Z

Museu i Centre d'Estudis de l'Esport
See A to Z

Museu Marítim
See A to Z

Museu Mentora Alsina
See A to Z, Gabinet de Física Experimental

Museu Militar
See A to Z, Montjuïc

Museu Monestir de Pedralbes
See A to Z, Pedralbes

Museu Ocenogràfic
(Museum of Oceanography)
Moll de Barcelona
E–08003 Barcelona
Tel. 3 18 77 49

Museu Odontològic de Catalunya
(Museum of Dentistry)

Carrer de la Tapineria 10
E–08002 Barcelona
Tel.3 10 15 55

Museu Picasso
See A to Z

Museu Tauri de la Monumental
See A to Z, Plaças de Toros, Monumental

Museu Tèxtil i d'Indumentària
See A to Z

Museu Verdaguer
See A to Z, Casa-Museu Verdaguer

Music

Palau de la Música	The most important concert building in the town is the Palau de la Música Catalana (See A to Z). In this magnificent modernist building both classical and modern experimental music is performed and jazz and pop concerts are held.
Liceu	The Liceu (See A to Z) is a first-rate opera house with its own orchestral ensemble. Concerts usually commence in November. Programme information tel. 3 01 87 96
Palau des Esports	The construction of the new Palau des Esports Sant Jordi has meant a change of purpose for the old sports palace (Carrer de Lleida 40). Nowadays it hosts rock and pop concerts with local and international groups. Programme information tel. 4 24 27 76
Other concert halls	The Caixa de Barcelona (Municipal Savings Bank) and the Caixa de Pensions (Pensions Bank) promote a number of cultural activities including musical events. Further information from branches of these banks.
Preview of events	The weekly guide to events "Guía del Ocio" is obtainable from all news kiosks. For programme information tel. 3 17 10 96 (Amics de la Música, Friends of Music).

Night Life

General	There is an abundance of entertainment in the evenings and at night in Barcelona, from theatrical performances and concerts to pop and rock, and more exotic attractions such as strip-tease. Full details are contained in the "Guia del Ocio" which is published weekly and which can be obtained from any newspaper kiosk or from hotel reception desks.

Opening Times

Museums, Sights	The opening times for the museums described in the Sights from A to Z are given in that section. However, these times may be subject to alteration

according to seasonal and other factors. In general it can be assumed that the amusement parks on Montjuïc and Tibidabo are only open at weekends in winter but open throughout the week in summer (except Montjuïc which is closed on Mondays).

As a rule museums are closed on Mondays.

There are no legally fixed shop opening hours in Spain. In general shops open on Monday to Saturday between 9 to 10am until 1 or 2pm and between 4 to 5pm until 8 or 8.30pm. In summer they often remain open later (especially food shops, tobacconists and some clothes shops).

Shops

The large stores and shopping centres are generally open Monday to Saturday from 10am to 8pm continuously. A few, however, close on Monday morning.

Department stores, shopping centres

Banks are open Monday to Friday between 9am and 2pm, Saturday 9am to 12.30 or 1pm. In tourist areas during the high season they sometimes open in the afternoon.

Banks

Hours when post offices open vary and generally are displayed in the offices. Most open on Monday to Saturday from 9am to 2pm. The central Post office in Plaça Antonio López is open Monday to Friday from 9am to 9pm and Saturday 9am to 2pm.

Post offices

Post

Post and telegram

General: The post office (correos) is responsible for mail, mail orders and telegrams, but not for the telephone network (this is operated by Telefónica; see Telephone).

Stamps: Stamps (sellos) are available from post offices and also from tobacconists (estancos) which remain open until late in the evening. These are recognisable by a sign which consists of a stylised yellow tobacco leaf and the letter T.

Letter boxes: International mail should be posted in letter boxes (buzones, singular buzon) marked "extranjero" (abroad).

Poste restante: Letters, parcels and other correspondence can be collected from all post offices. They must be labelled with the recipient's name, preceded by "Lista de Correos", the name of the town or village and the province in brackets. Identification such as a passport is required for collection.

Public Holidays

January 1st	Any Nou (New Year)	Official public holidays
January 6th	Reis Mags (Three Kings)	
March 19th	Sant Josep (St Joseph's)	
May 1st	Diada del Treball (Labour Day)	

167

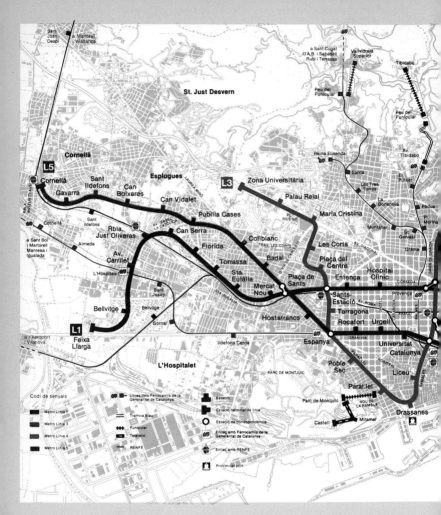

June 24th	Sant Joan (St John; king's name day)
June 29th	Sant Pere i Sant Pau (St Peter and St Paul)
July 25th	Sant Jaume (St James the Apostle)
August 15th	Assumpció (Feast of the Assumption)
September 11th	Diada Nacional de Catalunya (Catalonian National Feast Day)
September 24th	La Mercè (celebration of the city's patron saint)

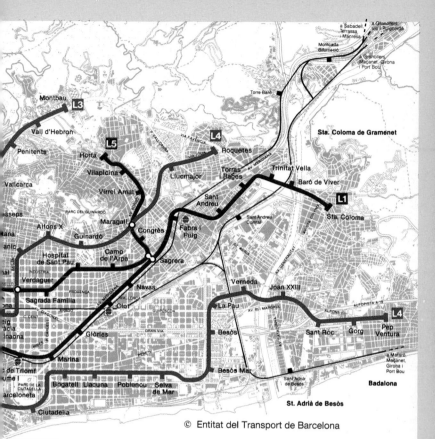

© Entitat del Transport de Barcelona

BARCELONA

October 12th	Diada de la Hispanitat (Discovery of America)
November 1st	Tots Sants (All Saints')
December 6th	Dia de la Constitució (Day of the Catalonian constitution)
December 8th	Immaculada Concepció (Annunciation)
December 25th	Nadal (Christmas Day)
December 26th	Sant Esteve (St Stephen)

Public Holidays

Movable public holidays	Good Friday Easter Monday Corpus Christi

Public Transport

Metro

General

Barcelona has an impressive and efficient Metro (underground railway system) which means that all the places of interest are accessible quickly and conveniently. It operates Mondays to Fridays between 5am and 11pm; Saturdays and Sundays on days preceding public holidays until 1am.

Fares

There is one standard fare for all single journeys; maps of the underground lines are on display at all stations. It is worth purchasing a multi-ticket (targeta multiviatge) or a one, two or three day ticket (abonament tempora) for an extended visit to Barcelona. A higher tariff of charges applies to single journeys at night, at weekends and on public holidays.

Ferrocarrils de la Generalitat de Catalunya (FF.CC.)

General

Certain Metro lines are continued beyond the Metro network by the Ferrocarrils de la Generalitat de Catalunya (Catalan Government Railways). They are the connections from the Plaça de Catalunya to the foot of Tibidabo and in the west of the town Pedrales and to Sant Cugat del Vallès, together with Plaça d'Espanya to L'Hospitalet de Llobregat. For information on services tel. 2 05 15 15.

Fares

Although the trains of the FF.CC. are hardly distinguishable from those of the Metro and they operate from the Metro stations Plaça de Catalunya, Plaça d'Espanya and Diagonal, there is no common fare system (except for some multi-journey and saver tickets) so it is necessary to purchase a new ticket when making these connections.

Buses

General

There are many inner-city bus lines operating from 5.30 or 6.30am to 9.30 or 10.30pm. For the tourist the "Bus 100 – Bus Turístic" service (see Sightseeing) is of particular interest. It operates from the end of June to mid-September; a "Discover Barcelona" ticket is valid for a half or whole day for unlimited travel on Bus 100, Tramvía Blau (blue train), Montjuïc funicular, Montjuïc telefèric and Tibidabo funicular.

Night buses (Nitbus)

There are eight special services operating late at night and in the early morning. They make frequent stops on the following routes:

N 1: Zona Franca (Free harbour zone) – Plaça de Catalunya

N 2: Collblanc – Plaça de Catalunya – La Verneda

N 3: Avinguda de Xile – Plaça de Catalunya – Montcada i Reixac

N 4: Plaça Catalana – Plaça de Catalunya – Passeig de la Vall d'Hebron

N 5: Plaça de Catalunya – Horta

N 6: Baró de Vivier – Plaça de Catalunya – Poligon Canyelles

N 7: Plaça de Catalunya – Besòs Mar

N 8: Plaça de Catalunya – Avinguda del Tibidabo

National Railways (RENFE)

RENFE, the nationalised railway company, operates railway services from
Sants station (see Railway Stations) to local destinations (airport and the
seaside resorts in the south of Catalonia).

Transports Metropolitans de Barcelona (TMB)

A map of all public transport routes (Guia del Transporte Público de Barce-
lona y su Area Metropolitana) is available from the Tourist Information
Offices (see Information) and from the Transports Metropolitans de Barce-
lona (TMB) at the Plaça de Catalunya, at the Ronda de Sant Pau (No. 43), at
Sants main station (see Railway Stations), at the Metro station Plaça de la
Universitat and other main Metro stations.

Information

TMB

Timetable information regarding TMB is available Monday to Friday
between 7.30am and 8.30pm and Saturdays between 8am and 2pm tel.
3 36 00 00.

Telephone
Information
Service

See entry

Taxis

Radio and Television

Spanish radio and television organisations have their headquarters in
Madrid. The Ràdio Associació de Catalunya (UKW 105.0 MHz) broadcasts
in July and August, from Monday to Friday, news programmes for foreigners in English at 10.30am.
In cases of extreme emergency the Spanish radio organisation Ràdio
Nacional will transmit messages for tourists travelling in Spain. The motoring associations can provide information.

Radio

Spanish television (Televisión Española; TVE) broadcasts on two channels:
TVE 1 (mostly in Castilian) and TVE2 (mostly in Catalan). In addition there
are two channels broadcasting local programmes in Catalonia, many of
which are in Catalan: TV3 (popular programmes) and Canal 33 (for specific
subjects).
Numerous hotels in Barcelona are connected with cable television offering
a wide range of programmes.

Television

Radio stations

Catalunya Música
UKW 101.5 MHz

Public radio

Radio and Television

Ràdio Associació de Catalunya
UKW 105.0 MHz

Radio Nacional de España
Radio 1: MW 738 KHz
Radio 2: UKW 93.0 MHz
Radio 3: UKW 98.5 MHz
Radio 4: UKW 100.8 MHz
Radio 5: MW 1107 KHz and UKW 88.7 MHz

Private stations   Radio Zona Franca
UKW 106.5 MHz

Onda Cero Radio
MW 621 KHz

Radio 80
UKW 90.7 MHz

Ràdio Antena 3
UKW 104.3 MHz

Ràdio Barcelona EAJ-1
MW 828 and UKW 93.9 MHz

Ràdio Dial Barcelona
UKW 99.4 MHz

Ràdio Miramar
MW 666 KHz

Ràdio Nova
UKW 100.0 MHz

Ràdio Pont Nou
UKW 99.4 MHz

Radio Popular de Barcelona
UKW 102.0 MHz

Ràdio RMK-7
UKW 107.5 MHz

Radio Salud
UKW 89.1 MHz

Radio Tiempo
UKW 94.9 MHz

Ràdio Tràfic
UKW 96.9 MHz

Television stations

Public stations   Televisión Española

Televisió Catalana

Antena 3 de Televisión

Canal Plus de Televisión

Telecinco

In total there are 10 local television stations, most of them transmitting on UHF channel 39.

Railways

The railway network in Spain is not so developed as in other central European countries but in Catalonia it is relatively close-meshed; it is constantly being upgraded and modernised. All larger towns can be reached by train. The main lines are from Portbou (border station for France) through the interior via Girona and close to the coast along the Costa Brava to Barcelona and from Puigcerdà (another border station for France) via Ripoll and Vic to Barcelona.

RENFE

Owing to the wider guage on Spanish main railway routes (1672mm) compared with the central European standard (1435mm) it is necessary to change trains at the French-Spanish border, with the exception of certain international trains with adjustable bogies (see also Getting to Barcelona, by train).

Railway information is available from the RENFE Central Information Bureau in Barcelona tel. 3 22 41 42; for 24-hour service tel. 4 90 02 02.

Central Information Bureau

The trains of FF.CC. (Ferrocarrils de la Generalitat de Catalunya) serve the region around Barcelona (e.g. via Sant Cugat del Vallès to Sabadell or Terrassa from the Plaça de Catalunya station; the Plaça d'Espanya to Montserrat line passes places of interest to the visitor). The FF.CC. also operates services to destinations inland (Tibidabo, Sarrià district).

FF.CC.

Central Information Bureau

FF.CC. central information bureau of tel. 2 05 15 15.

Railway Stations

There are two long-distance railway stations in Barcelona maintained by the nationalised railway company RENFE (Red Nacional de los Ferrocarriles Españoles).

RENFE

Trains heading north depart from the Estació Barcelona Terme-França (French station) on the north-eastern edge of the old town. It is currently undergoing renovation and extension. While this work is being carried out north-bound long-distance trains and trains to the airport depart from the station below the Plaça de Catalunya.

Barcelona central station is the Estació Sants, north-west of the Plaça d'Espanya. Long-distance national services to Madrid, Andalucía, Galicia,

Restaurants

Valencia, etc. and international trains (including daily services to Paris and Geneva) operate from here. Regional services to the seaside resorts of south Catalonia leave from this station. Trains stopping here also stop at the more centrally located Estacío Passeig de Gràcia, as well as Estació Plaça de Catalunya for connections to Vic, Puigcerdà and la Tour de Carol (for Andorra).

FF.CC.
The local railway network of the FF.CC. (Ferrocarrils de la Generalitat de Catalunya) operates from the station below the Plaça d'Espanya. There are services to Tibidabo via Sant Cugat del Vallès to Sabadell or Terrassa. Services to the south of Catalonia and to Montserrat operate from the Placa d'Espanya.

Railways
See entry

Restaurants

General
As everywhere else in Spanish tourist areas and cities Barcelona has a wide range of restaurants (restaurantes) to suit every palate.

Mealtimes
Meals in Spain are taken one to two hours later than in most other countries; hotel restaurants frequented principally by central European and British visitors often go to considerable trouble to meet the eating habits of their guests. There are also many restaurants serving hot food throughout the day.

Restaurants in Barcelona (selection)

Old Town
La Odisea, Carrer Copons 7
Aitor, Carrer Carbonell 5
Agut d'Avignon, Carrer Trinidad 3
Gran Café, Carrer Avinyó 9
La Cuineta, Carrer Paradis 4
Quo Vadis, Carrer del Carme 7
Senyor Parellada, Carrer Argenteria 37
Siete Puertas, Passeig d'Isabel II 14
Mediterráneo, Passeig Colom 4
Los Caracoles, Carrer Escudellers 14
L'Hogar Gallego, Via Laietana 5

New Town
*Reno, Carrer Tusset 27
*Via Veneto, Carrer Ganduxer 10
*Beltxena, Carrer Mallorca 275
Neichel, Avinguda de Pedralbes 16 bis
Azulete, Via Augusta 281
Botafumeiro, Carrer Gran de Gràcia 81
La Cupula, Carrer Teodor Roviralta 37
El Gran Colmado, Carrer Consell de Cent 318
37 Roux, Carrer Dr. Roux 37
El Túnel de Montaner, Carrer Sant Màrius 22
El Dorado Petit, Carrer Dolors Monserdá 51
La Dama, Avinguda Diagonal 423
Jaume de Provença, Carrer Provença 88
Ara-Cata, Carrer Doctor Ferràn 33
Bel Air, Carrer C-D8-rsega 286
Hostal del Sol, Passeig de Gràcia
Gorria, Carrer de la Diputació 421

Rias de Galicia, Carrer Lleida 7
Lluria, Carrer Roger de Lluria 23
Soley, Carrer Bailén 29
Casa Chus, Avinguda Diagonal 339 bis

Font del Gat, Passeig de Santa Madrona   Montjuïc

Safety Precautions

In the main season, especially in Barcelona and the other large centres of
tourism, an increase must be expected in thefts. Many a wallet has changed
hands in a crowd and the detection rate is small. Gypsies have, on occa-
sions, been active as pickpockets and confidence tricksters (a popular trick
is to place a carnation in the victim's lapel while calling out "Simpatia!")
and it is debatable which is the more remarkable: the sleight of hand or
their sheer audacity. It is advisable to avoid "games of chance" which are a
common sight on the Ramblas. Cars should not be parked in unsupervised
places.

The narrow streets of the Barri Gòtic and Barri Xino are best avoided after
dark, especially by unaccompanied persons.

If the police are informed of a theft or that something has been stolen from
a vehicle, the victim will be treated with courtesy but will have little chance
of any action being taken, for the authorities are simply overtaxed; however, a statement made to the police in the event of a complaint or a theft is
necessary to support a claim under insurance. A heavy police presence is
obvious in the centres of the drug scene (e.g. Plaça Reial and the Ramblas).
They are primarily concerned with preventing violent attacks.

It is advisable always to keep articles of value on the person (identity
documents, money, etc.) and to leave large sums of cash and cheques in
the hotel safe deposit or in a security box at a camp site. It is also a good
idea to have photocopies of passports and other important documents
which should be kept separately from the originals. In the event of loss this
will greatly facilitate replacement (see Travel Documents).

The loss of Eurocheques, travellers' cheques, credit and cheque cards, etc.,   Note
should be immediately reported to the bank or other issuing office in order
that replacements may be made available.

Shopping and Souvenirs

Spanish craftwork has a long tradition and products based on traditional
designs can be found as well as modern craftwork.

The antique shops are also to be found in the Old Town. A thorough   Antiques
knowledge of the subject is essential. Numerous antiquarian bookshops
are also situated here.

Barcelona is without doubt the centre of the Spanish book trade. Art and   Books
picture books make ideal souvenirs; for those proficient in Catalan and
Castilian there are books of fiction and poetry.

There is a particularly good selection of ceramic work on sale in many   Ceramics
places; in Catalonia most of this comes from the town of La Bisbal. Goods

aimed at the souvenir trade predominate; the everyday articles of the region are tasteful, practical and inexpensive. In Barcelona colourful decorative tiles painted in designs from the Museu de Ceràmica (see A to Z) are popular.

Glass

A typical souvenir of Barcelona is the artistic glassware; particularly the charming little ships in bottles made completely out of glass.

Jewellery

Spanish silverware is very attractive. In the better shops the visitor can find artificial pearls which cannot be distinguished from the real thing, expertly manufactured by the people of Mallorca. These pearls are certainly not cheap fashion jewellery and are sold not only in Spain but exported all over the world. The most noteworthy brand is "Perlas Majorica". Many jewellery shops are to be found in the Old Town.

Leather

Good modern leather work (shoes, clothing, accessories) can often be bought directly from the factory. On the Ramblas hawkers' prices should be regarded with due suspicion; there are numerous respectable specialist shops. Plenty of time should be allowed to compare quality and price. Shoes made in Spain can, of course, be obtained in the UK and the advantage in price of buying them in Spain is not very great.

Replicas

Replicas of the exhibits on display can also be obtained from many museums (e.g. Museu d'Art de Catalunya in the Palau Nacional, Museu de Ceràmica, Museu Arqueològic (see entries A to Z)).

Textiles

The textile industry in Barcelona is long-established. There is a correspondingly wide choice so it is advisable to seek the advice of the staff in the specialist shops.

Spirits

Spain has good and cheap spirits, principally brandy. This is distilled from wine and resembles cognac but is fruitier in taste and has a stronger aroma than its French counterpart. The best brands are "Duque de Alba", "Cardenal Mendoza", "Lepanto" and "Carlos I"; cheaper brands such as "Veterano Osborne" or "Carlos III" can also be obtained abroad. Aniseed liqueur is popular throughout the country and is drunk after meals – it makes the oily Spanish food more digestible.
For other details about Spanish drinks see Food and Drink and also Wine.

Sweets

Spanish sweets are popular souvenirs (including candied fruits, nougat and Turkish honey) some of which originated in the time of the Arab domination in Spain. The Moors were particularly fond of very sweet titbits, the taste of which is too strong for those from other countries. Ensaimadas, a sweet pastry made of light oatmeal dough and often with a filling, was originally a speciality of Mallorca; small ones are served for breakfast but larger ones can also be obtained. A visit to one of the larger patisseries is recommended.

Tip

A visit to the workshops and shops of the Poble Espanyol on Montjuïc provides a comprehensive picture of Catalonian craftwork. The numerous large department stores (Corte Inglés and Galerías Preciados) should not be overlooked.

Sightseeing

From the end of June to mid-September the "Barcelona Transports Turístics" operates a circular tour (no guide but information on the tourist bus) which departs from the Plaça de Catalunya and includes the following city sights:

Transports Turístics "Bus 100 – Bus Turístic" See logo p. 176

1. Plaça de Catalunya: Oficina de Turisme, Old University and Palau de la Música Catalana.

2. Passeig de Gràcia: Casa Milà, Casa Batlló, Casa Amatller, Casa Lleó Morera, Fundació Antoni Tàpies and Museu de la Música.

3. Sagrada Família: Temple de la Sagrada Familia, Avinguda Gaudí and Hospital de la Santa Creu i de Sant Pau.

4. Parc Güell: Museu Gaudí.

5. Parc de la Creuta del Coll.

6. Tibidabo: Museu de la Ciència, Tramvia Blau, Funicular and Parc d'Atraccions.

7. Monestir de Pedralbes.

8. Olympic Grounds Avinguda Diagonal: Plaça Pius XII, Palau Reial de Pedralbes (Ceramics Museum), Barcelona Football Club Stadium and Museum.

9. Estació Central de Sants: Parc de l'Espanya Industrial, Parc Joan Miró and Plaça dels Països Catalans.

10. Poble Espanyol: Poble Espanyol, Pavillon Mies van der Rohe, Palau Nacional (Museu d'Art de Catalunya; temporarily closed), Avinguda de la Reina Maria Cristina (illuminated fountains) and Trade Fair Grounds.

11. Anell Olimpic: Olympic Stadium, Palau Sant Jordi, Piscina Bernat Picornell (swimming stadium) and Universitat de l'Esport.

12. Montjuïc: Cog-railway and overhead cablecar, Parc d'Attractions, Fundació Joan Miró, Castell de Montjuïc, Museu Militar, Teatre Grec and Museu Arqueològico.

13. Monument a Colom and Rambles: Colombus Monument, Golondrines (harbour tour), Museu Marítim and Museu de la Cera.

14. Pla del Palau: Museu Picasso, Museu del Born and Parc de la Ciutadella (Zoo, Museu de Zoologia, Parlament de Catalunya, Museu d'Art Modern, Museu de Geologia).

15. Barri Gòtic: Plaça Sant Jaume, Casa de la Ciutat, Palau de la generalitat, Cathedral, Museu d'Història de la Ciutat, Plaça del Rei, Plaça Reial, Teatre del Liceu, Mercat de la Boqueria and Palau de la Vireina.

Visitors can travel around the city by tourist buses, the Tramvía Blau (Blue Tram), the funicular railway to Tibidabo and the cog and overhead railways to Montjuïc. A half-day or day ticket is available which includes unlimited use of the above means of transport.

An information brochure is obtainable from the municipal information bureaux (see Information) and TMB offices (see Public Transport, Information).

Taxis

General

Black and yellow taxis are a comfortable and still reasonably priced means of transport. As there are many taxi ranks they are easy to find. A free taxi can be hailed in the street (recognisable by the sign "libre" or "lliure" or a green light on its roof) or ordered by telephone 3 58 11 11, 3 30 08 04, 4 91 00 00 or 3 00 38 11. They are equipped with meters.

It is advisable to make a note of the exact address of the hotel and the nearest road junction to it as the name of the hotel alone is insufficient for even the most knowledgable taxi-drivers.

Supplements

Supplements are payable for waiting time, journeys between the centre and the airport, port and railway stations, and for carrying pets or larger pieces of luggage.

Telephone

Telephone codes:
From UK to Spain: 010 34 (+3 for Barcelona)
From US and Canada to Spain: 011 34 (+3 for Barcelona)
From Spain to UK: 07 (wait for second dialling tone) 44
From Spain to US and Canada: 07 (wait for second dialling tone) 1
From within Spain to Barcelona (city and province): 93

Telephone boxes:
Long-distance and international calls can be conveniently made from public coin-boxes. Instructions for use (usually in several languages) are posted. Coins of 25, 50 and 100 pesetas are required (the five peseta coin is only valid for use for calls within Spain!).
Telephone calls from the hotel are charged at a considerably higher rate than normal.

Theatre

Although there is no national theatre in Barcelona at present there are about twenty-five venues of various sizes. Theatres are situated in the districts of the Ramblas, Avinguda Parallel, Montjuïc, La Ribera and Passeig de Gràcia.

The far-reaching improvements taking place in the city include the Catalonian National Theatre on the Plaça de les Glòries. It will house two theatres and a concert hall with the auditorium (two concert halls with library and Museum of Musical Instruments) next door.

The weekly guide "Guía del Ocio" (in Spanish, but the essentials are recognisable) is obtainable from all news kiosks.

Programme of events

See Music

Opera

Time

During the winter months (October to March) mainland Spain and the Balearic Islands observe Central European Time, e.g. one hour ahead of Greenwich Mean Time: six hours ahead of Eastern Standard Time in the United States. During the summer months (April to the end of September) the clock is advanced by one hour. The exact dates are published in the press.

Tipping

Although in hotels and restaurants the service charge is included in the bill, it is usual to tip the waiter (camarero), chambermaid (camamera or muchacha) and other personnel (mozos), especially when some particular service has been provided. Waiters in restaurants expect 5 to 10% of the bill, but in bars less than 5% of the change received is sufficient.

Taxi drivers, usherettes at theatres, cinemas and bullfights expect a tip, so that it is advisable always to have some small change.

Trade Fairs

The trade fair grounds (Fira de Barcelona), situated between the Plaça d'Espanya and the Palau Nacional, are the largest in the country after Madrid. The trade centre is of international importance with over 40 international events taking place here annually.

General

Trade Fairs and Exhibitions (a selection)

BCN Hombre (menswear)
Caravaning (international caravan fair)
Pielespaña (national leather goods)

January

Equipal (international fair for office equipment; alternate years, 1993, etc.)

January/February

Barnajoya (international fair for watches and jewellery)

February

Expofryc (international refrigeration exhibition; alternate years, 1993, etc.)
TechnoAlimentaria (international food exhibition; alternate years, 1993, etc.)

February/March

Alimentaria (international food exhibition; alternate years, 1992, etc.)
Sport (winter and mountain sports equipment)

March

March/April	Saló d'Anticuaris (antiques fair)
April	Expomóvil (international exhibition for motor industry; alternate years, 1992, etc.) Mostra Tejidos (textiles) Rodatur (international tourism fair)
April/May	Construmat (international exhibition for the construction industry; alternate years, 1993, etc.)
May	International Automobile Fair (alternate years, 1993, etc.) Rehabitec (building restoration fair; alternate years, 1992, etc.)
June	Credern (business development fair; alternate years, 1993, etc.) Expotrónica (applied electronics) Feria Internacional de Barcelona (international fair for business and industry) Informat (information technology)
June/July	Liber (international book fair)
July	BCN Hombre (menswear)
September	Sonimag (international audio-visual electronics fair) Sport (sports and camping equipment)
September/ October	Barnajoya (international watch and jewellery fair) Mundifher (tools, DIY and garden equipment; alternate years, 1993, etc.) ExpoHogar (international gifts and household goods fair) Feria Española del Recreativo (national recreation and leisure fair)
October	Hostelco (international catering technology fair; alternate years, 1993, etc.) Inverfira (banking and finance; alternate years, 1993, etc.) Mostra Tejidos (textiles) Technoclinic (international fair for hospital equipment)
November	Expoaviga (international agricultural and cattle breeding fair; alternate years, 1993, etc.) Expominer (minerals and fossils) Exposalud (health and fitness) Nivalia (winter sports)
December	Sálon Nautico (international boating fair)
December/January	Festival de la Infancia y la Juventud (children's festival)

Travel Documents

Personal documents	Visitors from the United Kingdom, the United States, Canada, Australia and New Zealand must have a valid passport. No visa is required by nationals of Australia and New Zealand for a stay of up to one month, the UK and Canada for a stay of up to three months, and the United States for a stay of up to six months; provided in each case they are not taking up any paid

employment. An extension of stay can be granted by the Spanish police authorities. Children under 16 years of age require their own passport or else must be entered in one of their parent's passports.

A national driving licence is accepted in Spain if it is of the pink EC type, otherwise it must be accompanied by an official translation stamped by a Spanish consulate; it is probably easier and cheaper to carry an international driving permit (available from motoring organisations). The car registration document must be carried as well as an international insurance certificate (green card), and a bail bond (issued by an insurance company with green card) should be taken out, since in the event of an accident the car may be impounded pending payment of bail. The oval nationality plate is required. It is advisable to take out comprehensive insurance when hiring a vehicle as third party insurance in Spain only covers personal injury; a deposit is not usually necessary.

Car documents

An official vetinerary certificate including immunisation against rabies (translated into Spanish) is required for the importation of dogs and cats into Spain. Immunisation should not have taken place less than 30 days or more than one year prior to travelling.
In view of the strict quarantine regulations concerning the import of live animals into the United Kingdom, British visitors are advised to leave their pets at home.

Pets

It is advisable to prepare copies of passports, driving licence, E111, etc., before departure and to keep these separately from the originals. If papers are lost a photocopy makes it easier to obtain a replacement.

Note

Travel Regulations

See Motoring

When to go

The best time for visiting Barcelona is late spring and early summer or autumn. In high summer, during the school holidays, the place becomes so crowded that obtaining accommodation without pre-booking can be a problem. Summer heat is moderated by winds off the sea, but the air can become oppressive in parts of the inner city of Barcelona owing to emissions from cars and industry.

Wine

Although Spain has a greater acreage of vineyards than, for example, Italy or France it is of less importance internationally for wine production. However, export production is increasing and following Spain's entry into the European Community the classification system corresponds to European standards.

General

On the lower south-eastern slopes of the Pyrenees there are surprisingly very few vineyards and their produce has little importance outside the region. The largest wine-producing area of Catalonia is to the south of Barcelona, centred around Tarragona. Here the emphasis is on the production of red wine, the greater part of which is sold as blended wine. However, Catalonia is renowned for the production of sparkling wine.

Catalonian wine

Drinks   See Food and Drink

Youth Hostels

Young people will find reasonably priced accommodation in Youth Hostels (albergues juvenils). Members of national youth hostel organisations affiliated with the International Youth Hostels Association can normally use the hostels from July to September. For an individual a stay in a hostel is limited to three nights; in the high season previous booking is advisable.

Youth Hostel
Handbook

The International Youth Hostel Handbook (volume 1 for Europe and the countries bordering the Mediterranean) is issued every year and is available in Britain from: YHA Mail Order Department, YHA Adventure Shops, 14 Southampton Street, London WC2E 7HY.

Youth Hostel in
Barcelona centre

Hostal de Joves de la Ciutadella
(at the Parc de la Ciutadella)
Passeig Pujades 29
E–08018 Barcelona
Tel. 3 00 31 04

Other youth
hostels

Alberg de Montserrat
(in Gràcia district)
Carrer Mare Déu Coll 41–51
E–08023 Barcelona
Tel. 2 13 86 33 and 2 10 51 51

Alberg Kabul
(in the Old Town)
Plaça Reial 17
E–08029 Barcelona
Tel. 3 18 51 90

Alberg Pere Tarrés
(in Les Corts district)
Carrer Numància 149
E–08029 Barcelona
Tel. 4 10 23 09

Alberg Studio
(in Sarrià-Sant Gervais)
E–08034 Barcelona
Tel. 2 05 09 61

Index

Notes

Notes